# GREER

## FROM COTTON TOWN TO INDUSTRIAL CENTER

*SNOWBALL FIGHT. J. Verne Smith, wife Lillian, and friends exchange rounds in a snowball fight in front of the Greer Methodist meetinghouse around the turn of the century.*

## DEDICATION

For my girls, Delaine, CarraLea, and Abigale, for Pete, and in memory of my parents whose lives were windows to the past.

~ Ray Belcher

This book is dedicated to my husband Alan, who for 37 years has been my loving encourager. It is also dedicated to our children: our daughter Alison Hiatt Carpenter, who has made us proud; our son-in-law Roger, who is like a son; and to the memory of our son Jack Andrew, who was always ready for a new challenge and would have loved that his mother took on this one.

~ Joada Palmer Hiatt

THE
MAKING OF AMERICA
SERIES

# GREER

## FROM COTTON TOWN TO INDUSTRIAL CENTER

RAY BELCHER AND JOADA P. HIATT

ARCADIA
PUBLISHING

ISBN 978-0-7385-2420-7

Published by Arcadia Publishing,
Charleston, South Carolina

Printed in the United States of America

Library of Congress control number: 2003100761

For all general information contact Arcadia Publishing at:
Telephone 843-853-2070
Fax 843-853-0044
E-Mail sales@arcadiapublishing.com
For customer service and orders:
Toll-Free 1-888-313-2665

Visit us on the Internet at www.arcadiapublishing.com

Front cover: *From a start of 100 acres each, given to them by their father, Robert A. and Isham Benjamin Dobson created an agri-business partnership during the 1920s. Engaging in cotton growing, peach and grain farming, ginning, and fertilizer manufacture, they increased their holdings to over 2,200 acres. Pictured with farmhands is Isham "Benny" Dobson during a 1930s grain harvest.*

# CONTENTS

# ACKNOWLEDGMENTS

The authors express appreciation to those excellent interviewees who suffered many questions and often times repeated visits. Many of those who contributed so much information toward this project have since become a portion of history themselves. The following were gracious enough to give interviews and remember the stories of Greer: Geneva Ashmore, Carl Belcher, Carrabell C. Belcher, David L. Belcher, Ernest Belcher, Grady L. Belcher, John V. Belcher, Susie Belcher, Bob Blackwell, Harley Bonds, Frank Carman, Alliene Cates, Atlee Chastain, Henry Clark, Mrs. Oscar Collins, R. Broughton Colvin, Talmadge Crisson, John C. Curry, Wilma Curtis, Constance Dillard, Palmer Dillard, Clyde Dobson, Leonard Dobson, Lawrence Earle, Oda Fowler, B.L. Frick, Faris Green, Frank Green, James D. Grubbs, Minnie Grubbs, Harper Hawkins, Vernon Hawkins, G. Hayes, Richard Hemphill, Luther Hester, Nell Hinkle, Minnie K. Hollingsworth, O.T. Holloway, Press Holtzclaw, Alton Howard, James C. Howard, Rometta Howard, Rob Hughes, Katie Johnson, J.L. Jones, Clarence Kimbrel, Mrs. T.A. Long, Quillan Lewellen, Lib Mayfield, Thomas McAbee, Ruth McAlister, Troy McAlister, John L. McMurray, Connie Miller, Jim Miller, Edmund Mosteller, Hendrix Mosteller, L.C. Pearson, William J. Pennington, Lewis Phillips, Grady Powell, D.C. Price, Henry and Francis Sammons, Russell Sheriff, Virginia Smith, Dan Stepp, David Bunyon Stone, Croel Suddeth, Florence Tucker, Mrs. R.B. Vaughn, Bertha Wentz, and Sybil West.

Alton Howard, Judith McDowell, Gayle White, Jerry Bryant, Bob Howard, Constance Dillard, and Norman Dukes provided certain research data that was extremely helpful in writing this account of Greer. Thomas A. McAbee provided extensive photographic services for this project. Carra and Pete Selent provided computer services and technical assistance.

For assistance in locating materials, the authors express gratitude to the staff of the South Carolina Room and Reference Department of the Greenville County Library, the Greenville County Law Library, Furman University Library Special Collections, Strom Thurmond Institute of Clemson University, the South Carolina State Library, and the South Caroliniana Library of the University of South Carolina.

The authors are also indebted to those individuals and organizations that provided pictures and other illustrations portraying Greer's history, including

Thomas and Doris McAbee, James Paget, Lucie Williams Robinson, William Robinson, Hampton-Lee Chapter of the United Daughters of the Confederacy (Chapter 1281), Francis Farmer Jones, Myra "Mack" Mason, Meda Land, Herbert Taylor, Greer First Bapist Church, Jean Smith Library of Greer, Shirley Beacham, Abbie Frick McWilliams, Evelyn Mason, Beatrice Whitman, Henry and Francis Sammons, Preston Johnson, Senator Verne Smith, Susan H. Young, Richard and Karolyn Taylor, Clyde and Anne Dobson, Mary Lee Landford, Homer Turner, Bobby Howard, Julia Martin, James and Linda Suber, Brenda Jolley, L.B. Rogers, Ruth Bishop, Sylvia Pitts, Nancy Simmons, Washington Baptist Church, and Patricia Chambers.

*LLOYD HUNT AWARDS DOBSON FAMILY. Lloyd Hunt presents an award to the Dobson family during Peach Festival activities. Shown are, from left: Leonard Dobson, Roy Dobson, Mrs. R.A. Dobson, Clyde Dobson, Lloyd Hunt, Connie Burnside, Lawrence Dobson.*

# INTRODUCTION

Greer, South Carolina is a New South town straddling the Greenville-Spartanburg county line. Named for a man who never lived within its city limits, Greer has had unique challenges based on its location. The happenstance of an early Native American boundary line and a railroad's choice of a site for its depot marked Greer history forever.

Like hundreds of similar towns stretching across the cotton belt of the South, Greer originated as a settlement on the edge of an antebellum plantation, part of a land grant issued to a soldier of the American Revolution. The strong and deeply religious Scotch Irish Presbyterians who peopled the area would produce families who would have vision and stamina to build a community some 100 years later. Three decades after the death of upstate plantation owner Hugh Bailey, William Shumate purchased the northern 200 acres of Bailey's property as an investment when he learned of plans for a railroad through the section. Shumate, like other visionaries of the era, perhaps foresaw the nature of the changes that were about to envelop the upstate.

Cotton was being sold in cotton-starved markets for its all-time highest prices, recommending to farmers, particularly the yeoman class, abandonment of subsistence agriculture in favor of producing cash crops. Two distinct factors favored this scenario: first, a railroad through the interior section of the South would provide a means to ship cotton to market, and import staple and fancy goods to general merchants; second, the successful use of phosphates by low country farmers encouraged their up country brethren to experiment with fertilizers. Appropriately, in early 1873, when the Airline Railway was completed and the first trains crawled from the eastern terminus through Greer's Depot, the first delivery of freight to the town-to-be was a load of fertilizer destined for three local cotton farmers.

From an inauspicious beginning, Greer's Depot, as it was called for another 20 years (and, by old timers, "Greer's" well into the twentieth century), slowly grew to prominence as a trading center. Like a rowdy frontier boom town in the Old West, its adolescence was characterized by no little degree of alcohol-induced violence, but at the same time, it gradually matured into a successful commercial, trading, and industrial center within 50 years of its origin. To that success, it owed contributions of farmers, merchants, and mill hands. Greer was progressive during the national age of Progressivism; it was patriotic in time of war. Along with the rest of the country, Greer struggled when the Great Depression closed its mills.

Roosevelt's New Deal changed agriculture and the cotton industry forever. Regulation and other forms of market manipulation, necessarily desperate measures for a desperate time, discouraged small-time farming operations. Textile competition from abroad, coupled with the United States' inability to protect the industry, led to the collapse of small corporations and/or consolidation with larger companies. Signaling nothing less than the closure of an era, two related but unmarked events occurred within months of each other during the early 1980s: Dobson's Gin processed its last cotton before the machinery was scrapped, and the last operating cotton mill closed its doors, ending a continuous chain of textile production that began in 1896.

For a time, Greer threatened to "wither on the vine." The central business sector along Trade Street and Poinsett Street was already in serious decline. The older, long-established groceries, dry goods stores, jewelers, and photographers had either closed or moved to newer locations on Wade Hampton Boulevard, the major Highway 29 linking Greenville and Spartanburg. With fewer of the newer enterprises along that route sporting a business sign with "Greer" in the title, the city faced the ignominy of virtual anonymity in the shadows of its neighbors. The process of McDonaldization had set in.

It wasn't the first time Greer had faced adversity. During the 1920s, when the boll weevil threatened to decimate the cotton farms, merchants and farmers worked together to maintain the integrity of the local cotton market. The chamber of commerce introduced, through seminars and meetings, successful alternative forms of agriculture, including dairy farming and peach growing. Greer transformed itself from cotton center to peach center by the late 1950s, attracting occasional national attention with its Peach Festival. During the next two decades, it attracted several small but diverse industrial operations, which provided jobs and guaranteed continued commerce as the town changed. Sluggish for a decade, Greer finally secured a replacement for the cotton industry when state leaders persuaded German manufacturer Bavarian Motor Works (BMW) to locate its first American plant just south of the city limits.

Greer has always been more than the sum of its commerce and industry. Greer is its people: devout, industrious, independent, sometimes colorful. Two major league ball players had Greer ties; Flint Rhem came to Greer to live after pitching for the St. Louis Cardinals for ten seasons, and Dennis Smith, known as the "Greer Peach," played for the 1937 New York Yankees. Greer has had two Miss South Carolinas; Jeanna Raney, Miss Greater Greer, won the title in 2001 and Danielle Davis of Greer was also Miss South Carolina in 1999 after she competed as Miss Williamston. Yet, the backbone of the community has been its solid hardworking citizens whose names are not found in history books. They continue to fill many churches of various faiths on Sundays and the high school football stadiums on Friday nights to see teams that have won state championships.

Provincial, back-home Greer of earlier days has disappeared in deference to a sprawling town struggling to stabilize its fiscal self while holding on to a sense of community identity. Yet, common threads still link the past and the present. Senator J. Verne Smith Jr. serves in the South Carolina Legislature today, while he continues the tradition of doing business in downtown Greer, operating the Tire Exchange. Like his father of early peach farming days, he works to promote his community. The lessons of history can be instructive in this effort to preserve continuity. Greer has a rich and fascinating heritage. The leadership of the city today and tomorrow must avoid the errors of the past and continue to reinvent its many successes for continued and prosperous longevity.

*SENATOR J. VERNE SMITH. Greer native Verne Smith, South Carolina state senator, represents the commitment to community that characterizes Greer to this day.*

# 1. Origins of Greer: Prehistory to 1873

Greer, South Carolina is located on the line that separates Greenville and Spartanburg Counties. After conflicts arose between settlers and Native Americans, who viewed their presence as encroachment into Indian land, a survey established the boundary between the Cherokee and the English. The line marked the beginning of Cherokee hunting grounds and extended the width of Greenville and Pickens Counties as wild land, buffering Cherokee towns further west. These lands were uninhabited when the first settlers made their way to the boundary and constructed farms and homes at the extreme limit of the frontier. After the boundary was established, the Cherokee had only two decades during which to hunt the vanishing deer before the American Revolution became the device by which the final corner of South Carolina became open to settlement.

After the Revolution, the state government created a land commission to allot the territory to veterans and others. No evidence of historical era Native American villages was discovered from the boundary to the Saluda River. Early farmers and plantation owners, however, in turning the pristine ground, discovered evidence of hunting and inhabitation from centuries long past. During Greer's farming era from the end of the Revolution until the 1970s, tillers of the soil continued to find and preserve a seemingly limitless number of ancient artifacts attesting to the area's suitability for life in primitive times.

Artifacts found in the area of greater Greer indicate that many ancient peoples, solitary hunters, seasonally migrating family/tribal groups, and perhaps permanent residents, were here as early as 9,000 to 10,000 years ago. Specific styles of stone and clay artifacts, which are plentiful in the area, vary in antiquity and suggest the local environment offered native people sufficient food, water, and security from enemies at least sporadically from the late Paleolithic Era through the Archaic and well into the historic era. Archeologists and advanced artifact collectors have confirmed the approximate age of specimens collected around Greer, but no comprehensive dig has been conducted except to determine the archeological potential of land about to undergo industrial development.

A complete record of the ancient Greer area does not exist; however, before wide interest in archeological preservation, local farmers, strolling the edges of their fields after rains, found evidence of native inhabitants. Henry K. Clark and Clarence Kimbrell, who farmed lands north and west of Greer during the 1920s through the 1970s, found and collected hundreds of artifacts, including stone axes, celts, projectile points, and pottery fragments. In 1969, Gordon Moon, Clark's neighbor whose home was located on the west bank of Frohawk Creek, discovered a massive natural stone mortar weighing 400 pounds which he and Clark pulled by tractor from the north end of his field. The stone was for grinding corn and perhaps nuts during the most recent cultural era. Its presence, along with other artifacts of recent manufacture, suggests a perennial campsite or village may have been located nearby. Taken together, the collections of Clark, Kimbrell, Moon, and others represent three great eras of at least partial inhabitation well within what today are the city limits of Greer. These eras are the Paleo, ranging to 8,000 years before the present day; the Archaic Period extending to the arrival of Europeans on the continent; and the Historical Era.

The largest concentration of artifacts was discovered only two decades ago along the South Tyger River lands used by farmers and others for over two centuries. During the 1930s, hunters found the broad river bottoms of the three branches of the Tyger River excellent rabbit-hunting land. The broadest plain near Greer was on the South Tyger and was popularly known as the Devil Catcher Swamp for its vines, mires, and mysterious cave-like holes at the base of a rise on the eastern bank. Approximately 3 miles north of Greer, the plain, abandoned by farmers for decades to the waterway, grew thick with river birch, alder, and muscadine, obscuring from vision and memory two prominences, one on each side of the

*PROJECTILE POINTS. Representing distinct prehistoric cultural eras dating to 7000 B.C., these artifacts were collected in 1980 from the construction site of Lake Robinson, Greer's principal water source.*

river, which rose up 20 and 50 feet, respectively, from the sandy bottom. Known as the "tater hills" by farmers when the bottoms were cleared for crops and avoided by rabbit hunters lest their dogs fall into holes near their bases, the hills were forgotten until the construction of Lake Robinson. When the initial land clearing began in late 1980, the clear cutting attracted the attention of artifact collectors. A severe drought dropped the river level to less than 3 feet in the deepest spots, draining the boggy areas and making accessible the entire plain. Before the clearing of the "tater hills" themselves, two professors from the University of South Carolina examined the site. Because of the suddenness with which the hills rose from the plain, there was a possibility the spot was a Mississippian cultural site, the hills being man-made mounds. Excavation revealed the hills to be natural formations; however, hundreds of artifacts were found on their surrounding summits, slopes, and wide plains.

The variety of projectile points found at the general site represented the greatest timeframe of any Greer area artifact found. One Paleo point of indistinct attribution was found 3 feet deep on the eastern hill and, as far as is known, all other artifacts were Archaic Era or later. Many of the projectile points were of the Morrow Mountain Type II, which may have been used 6,000 to 7,000 years ago. Other points include Savannah River type and indeterminate spike types. Many hundreds of chips were found near the western hill, which also had a quartz vein running east to west near its base. Quartz crystals of 1 inch or less were plentiful. Chips and the presence of quartz suggest the smaller western hill may have been a stone-knapping site.

Unfortunately, a systematic exploration of the "tater hills" site was never undertaken. The construction phase of the project was underway before amateurs discovered its potential archeological significance. The clearing of the trees disrupted the soil severely, eliminating any useful stratigraphic data; nor were all artifacts kept together. A number of collectors visited the area over the several months the land was exposed to the elements before the reservoir was filled.

Greer artifact collectors have discovered other smaller sites over the years and have shared much of that information. From the body of artifacts found in the Greer area and the plentiful water supply in the form of rivers, creeks, and springs, Greer was at least frequently visited by peoples for a millennium and was the site of settlement from time to time for indeterminate periods.

The majority of minor sites where several artifacts were found, related by stratigraphy and/or type, are north of Greer, although two ancient (Paleo) sites have been identified, one east of the city and one to the southeast. A single point located near the intersection of Gap Creek Road and U.S. Highway 29 in Spartanburg County was identified as Dalton Type, dating to 8,000 years ago. Morrow Mountain Type II points and a celt were found by Clarence Kimbrell in his field at the intersection of Ansel School Road and Memorial Drive Extension, which is now the site of a residential development.

A stone-knapping site was located on the summit of a small hill nearby on Campbell Lake Road off U.S. Highway 14 North. This site is now a mobile home community. Sandy Flat/O'Neal native and widely known educator and syndicated genealogist Leonardo Andrea found artifacts at the summit of William W. Burgess's hilltop peach orchard and believed there was a village site at what today is the Burgess Hills development. A knapping site and possible quarry were located on the southern end of Palmer Dillard's farm off Buncombe Road. A rock mass was broken up when he had the land prepared for peaches early in the 1920s. Found nearby were projectile points, which Dillard said could be picked up by the "pocketfuls."

In the Frohawk Creek vicinity, Henry Clark collected stone axes, hoes, and projectile points, mostly from the Archaic Era. A few points have been found along a creek in Greer Mill village, in a vacant lot one block off the main street, and in the old Camp Highland Civilian Conservation Corps (CCC) campsite. Single points have been picked up at numerous spots where surface water runoff continually washes soil down slopes. These sites are so numerous in the general area that they cannot be individually identified.

One of the most recently found pieces of evidence of prehistoric native life in Greer surfaced during the early 1990s at the site of construction of the BMW plant. State archeologists were asked to evaluate evidence of prehistoric settlement in accordance with the state's antiquities law. What they found was not a particularly significant site in terms of size; an ancient Paleolithic hearth, confirming the goodness and utility of the land both then and now, was uncovered in their search.

In addition to artifacts, there was other lasting evidence of ancient people when the white men arrived to settle the area, such as the trading paths and trails, which led from the mountains to the sea and crisscrossed the Carolinas, intersecting other paths connecting the southern peoples with those to the west and the north. Ancient when the Europeans arrived, these trails served as highways into the hinterlands for explorers, traders, and settlers. These paths joined villages and stretched out into the network of trails that was used by native peoples for trading and warring purposes for hundreds or even thousands of years. Spaniards Hernando DeSoto and Juan Pardo followed these well-established paths. Pardo's expedition marched near present-day Inman in 1567. Later English explorers and colonists found the trails convenient for getting to and from watering and trading sites and locating forts and outposts. The Blackstock Road, Buncombe Road, and Highway 11 all originated as Native American paths.

The first Europeans to pass through this area were treasure seekers, followed by traders and deer skinners. Traders loaded goods on packhorses and carried them to exchange with the Native Americans. They swapped a variety of simple wares, including clay pipes, beads, brassware, steel tools, and cloth for deerskins. Permanent colonial settlement followed the traders by the mid-1700s. The pressure of settlers moving along a vaguely defined frontier border created tension with the Cherokee that escalated into war on the frontier in 1760. When the war ended the next year, the British proclaimed a boundary (not immediately surveyed) to placate the Indians. The boundary became an official part of the new British Imperial policy in 1763.

*GOOD WATER, CHICK'S SPRINGS. The health benefits of drinking natural spring water peaked for Chick's Springs by the turn of the century. Water was bottled and sold and later used as a basis for Ponder's Ginger Ale.*

The actual Native American boundary surveyed was more restrictive of white settlement than the proclamation line announced in 1763, and was surveyed in two separate projects by North and South Carolina. The North Carolina survey established the boundary line that ran due north from the Saluda River to Tryon Mountain, essentially the same line in use today separating Greenville and Spartanburg Counties. The North Carolina survey was completed by mid-July 1767. By that time, some whites had penetrated several miles into Native American lands. White encroachment prior to 1760 had led to war; afterwards, however, some whites were tolerated west of the border, one of the best known being Richard Pearis, who acquired an estate from the Lower Cherokee, about 1770, surrounding the mountain that bears his name. Jacob Hite, a Virginian and an associate of Richard Pearis, bought a tract from Pearis located near the crossing of the Old Spartanburg Road and Enoree River, about 2.25 miles from latter-day Bailey's Crossroads. Hite arrived with his family sometime after November 1775.

Neighbors to the Hites, although miles away, were the Hampton family. Just east of the present city limits of Greer lived Anthony Hampton, great-grandfather of the Confederate general Wade Hampton. He had arrived at the limit of settlement from North Kent, Virginia, in 1774 and founded a small settlement composed largely of the families of his adult children. The Hamptons and the neighboring Cherokee of the Lower Towns initially enjoyed a peaceful relationship, Cherokee visiting the Hampton settlement on occasion to trade.

When the American Revolution began in the North in mid-April 1775, many South Carolinians had already taken sides. Tories, supporters of the king, were numerous in the western part of Ninety-Six District. The Whigs, supporters of the Revolution, were concentrated in the Spartan District. By summer 1776, skirmishes had taken place near Ninety-Six and at the Great Canebrake. Also by this time, both Whigs and Tories had tried to secure a Native American alliance or at least their neutrality. For security, settlers near the boundary had constructed a line of small forts or fortified homesteads from Tryon, site of a blockhouse fort, to Pennington's, some two days ride to the south. Earle's and Gowan's Forts offered protection for the northern part of the district. Forts near present-day Greer were Fort Prince to the east of Hampton's farm and Wood's Fort, which may also have been known as Thompson's Station, located near the boundary line about 2 miles northeast of the center of present-day Greer.

In May 1776, two of Anthony Hampton's sons, Preston and Edward, as representatives of the frontier settlers and possibly as agents acting on behalf of low country patriots, went to the Cherokee to attempt to persuade them to remain neutral or else join the Whigs. Instead of persuading them, the Hampton brothers were made prisoners on May 17 at the order of Alexander Cameron, a British agent already at the lower Cherokee settlements. Cameron released the Hamptons after they swore an oath of neutrality.

The Hampton brothers returned to prepare the frontier settlements for possible war. Meanwhile, Native Americans from the Ohio River Valley who supported the king visited the Cherokee of Tennessee to urge them to remain loyal to the king as well. When it was clear that the majority of the Cherokee would make war in the name of the king, Cameron asked them to spare any loyalists living on the frontier or within the boundary. According to tradition, loyalists were to erect a peeled pole wrapped with white cloth in their yards to denote that war parties should not harm these homes. Known as the "pass over," this system did not work.

News of Native American attacks in the west alerted South Carolinians to the danger. To prevent a surprise attack, Preston Hampton, in mid-June 1776, led a group of militia to the mountains to seize Alexander Cameron. According to one account, Hampton was killed, along with four of his men, in this failed attempt. By the end of June, Native Americans and Tories had spread terror along the boundary line and eastward almost to Spartanburg. One source described the events of June and July as a single campaign of a war party made up of Tories and Native Americans that formed at Richard Pearis's plantation. From there, it methodically swept over a wide area along the frontier line.

The Hites, who had chosen to support the Patriot cause, were among those slain inside the boundary line. After killing James Hite, son of Jacob, some distance from his home, the raiding party descended upon the Hite household, killed Jacob, kidnapped his wife, and either kidnapped or killed his three daughters. From there, the war party split into two groups, one part turned south, killed the daughter of Nathaniel Austin near Guilder's Creek, and proceeded to attack

Lyndly's Fort where they were repulsed. The second group went to the Hampton settlement.

John Bynum, a grandson of Anthony Hampton's and the only survivor of the Hampton massacre, described the attack. Son of Margaret Hampton and Gray Bynum, seven-year-old John was staying with his grandparents. Edward Hampton had gone to warn his father-in-law, Bayliss Earle, of an impending attack. Edward's sister Elizabeth and her husband James Harrison sent their older children to alert the neighbors while they remained nearby to attend to outside chores. Their baby was left in the house with its grandparents. Brothers Henry and Wade were away from home when the attack came. Preston's wife and children were at their nearby home.

Bynum related that Anthony Hampton opened the door to the Native Americans when he saw them approach, extending a hand in peace as was his custom. A rifle fired and Preston Hampton fell to the ground. The elder Hampton and his wife were tomahawked where they stood. The Harrison infant was pulled from its bed and dashed against the wall of the house. Young Bynum was threatened, but spared and taken prisoner. The house was set afire. The Harrisons heard the commotion and arrived in time to find the house in flames, whereupon they retreated and hid in the woods until the Native Americans left.

According to a different account, Elizabeth Harrison had gone to visit a neighbor, a Mrs. Sadler, and had witnessed the attack from a hiding place. When it was safe, the women rode to Wood's Fort for help. An account of the massacre attributed to Benjamin F. Perry describes the Harrison flight as a 30-mile ride to a frontier fort where, with reluctance, a rescue party was allowed to return to the Hampton settlement. The Hampton and Wood's Fort sites have been memorialized with markers and extensively researched, although their exact locations have not yet been determined. Ansel Hawkins researched the fort's location when he was commander of the Greer American Legion Post and found evidence of several other community forts or fortified homes near the old boundary line in the Greer area.

By the time help arrived, the war party was gone, but not before it stopped at Preston Hampton's house, killed his children, and abused his wife—she never recovered her wits. According to the Reverend Robert H. Reid, founder of Reidville and student of Revolutionary history, the war party continued into the Spartan District, killing and scalping a number of people before turning northward into what now is Polk County, North Carolina, where the Hannon family was killed.

The reaction of the settlers was immediate. Men of the borderland formed militias, elected their leaders, and pursued the Native Americans. The Battle of Round Mountain, North Carolina ended the frontier uprising along the boundary line in the summer of 1776. Here, a youthful Captain of Militia Thomas Howard led his men to a surprise attack against a band of Tories and Native Americans camped just inside North Carolina. The aid of a Cherokee patriot named Skyucca

*WASHINGTON CHURCH. The Washington Community north of Greer was settled shortly after the Revolutionary War. The church family portrait shown dates to 1900 or earlier.*

insured the success of the attack. Ultimately, Skyucca's help cost him his life; he was later captured and killed by those whom he helped defeat. While the battle of Round Mountain quelled the immediate threat of Native American attack on the frontier, the Indians and Tories remained a threat until decisively defeated.

A force commanded by Colonel John Thomas of Fairforest and Colonel Ezekiel Polk of North Carolina pursued the war party. The Native Americans and Tories retreated, killing some of their prisoners, including the wife of Jacob Hite; her body was found at an abandoned Indian camp in mid-July. Thomas captured Richard Pearis's family and burned his trading post.

Edward Hampton was elected captain of a militia company and participated in the defense of the upcountry, distinguishing himself in battle until he was killed by Tories under the command of William "Bloody Bill" Cunningham. In late July, a large force under the command of Colonel Andrew Williamson marched from Charleston in response to the raids, destroying Cherokee towns and settlements in retaliation. Henry Hampton, who was among this troop, reported killing an Indian with his own hands who was wearing the coat of his slain brother Preston. By August 13, 1766, the lower towns were destroyed. The militia was demobilized in October. A treaty with the Native Americans was signed at DeWitt's Corner on May 7, 1777. For the remainder of the Revolution, the battles were small and few in the area near present-day Greer.

When the former Native American lands became available, veterans of the Revolution were among the first to settle the area that would become Greer. Captain Charles Bruce, Colonel John Thomas, and Henry Hughes were among the most prominent early settlers of the area. Attracted by the rich, fertile lands, farmers and land speculators migrated from the northern ridges of Virginia and Pennsylvania.

By the late 1790s, a well-worn wagon road connected the villages of Spartanburg and Greenville, intersecting the Native American path running north and south along the former Indian Boundary Line, by this time known as the "Old Boundary Line." Designated a postal road by the embryonic federal government, it was an important source of travel and communication for the area. The crossroads would become quite significant to the development of the area. With time, the north-south axis came to be called the Buncombe Road with its terminus at Asheville.

The site of the crossroads, just west of the Indian Boundary Line, was part of a grant of 500 acres made to Revolutionary War veteran Henry Hughes on February 5, 1787 for the sum of 11 pounds, 13 shillings, and 2 pence. Nearby

*THE CUNNINGHAMS. This family was one of the earliest families to settle on the "good land" near the Indian Boundary Line after the American Revolution. The photo shows a third Greer generation about 1908. The children include Ruth, Nelle, and R. Lee; the mother is Lillie Burnette Cunningham.*

parcels were distributed rapidly as a steady influx of settlers arrived from points north and south. Prominent among these was a group of Virginians from Culpepper County, including families of Cunninghams, Hammetts, Morgans, and Holtzclaws. Henry Hughes kept his property intact until 1798 when he sold it to John McDade. The property was further divided, coming into the hands of James Vernon, Hugh Bailey, Robert Greer, Phillip Lester, and others. Of the later owners of the Hughes's tract, it was Lester who owned the crossroads and made it a center of commerce for the next 15 years.

Phillip Crymes Lester was born in Lunenburg, Virginia on April 14, 1794, to Archibald and Elizabeth Crymes Lester. His parents migrated to Greenville County along with several other families shortly after 1800, where, on October 16, 1817, he married his first cousin Nancy Crymes. Two months later, Lester bought a tract from James Vernon from the Hughes grant containing 100 acres, including the crossroads and the Culbertson homestead. Here Lester made his home, planted fruit trees, farmed, built a tavern, conducted business, and expanded his ventures into the area's first cotton mill. When Lester arrived, much of the virgin woodland remained from ancient times. To Lester, the site where open forest yielded to the crossroads was a "pleasant grove," a name that was legally applied the next year when a post office was established on June 24, 1818, with him as its first postmaster.

*PLEASANT GROVE, FIRST CHURCH. A group of Baptists organized Pleasant Grove Baptist Church in 1833 in response to protracted effects from a revival that "broke out" at Brushy Creek Church in 1831, a part of a national religious phenomenon known as the second "Great Awakening." This first building was located just west of Bailey's Crossroads.*

*PLEASANT GROVE, SECOND CHURCH. Pleasant Grove was chartered under Act 2726 on December 20, 1837. The first land in possession of the church was a parcel of 1.6 acres deeded by Hugh Bailey in 1833 that provided a permanent site for the meetinghouse and much of the cemetery. The first meetinghouse was replaced by the one shown here.*

When Lester bought his first land, Buncombe Road had remained unchanged for centuries. It had served as a route for war parties, English adventurers, traders, and even Spanish conquistadors. The second decade of the nineteenth century saw a need for more and better roads, bridges, and other internal improvements to promote the South Carolina economy and connect with the rest of the new nation. In 1818, the state legislature authorized the construction of a state road, a branch of which would pass through Greenville District to the North Carolina line. When the road was in place, it entered the district from the south and connected with the Native American path through Pleasant Grove, assuring the tiny community of perpetual existence and prosperity.

Location was one factor in Lester's success. Buncombe Road served as a droving trail from the mountains to the markets south, and Lester's tavern provided a needed place of respite and refreshment. Lester's prosperity was such that he was able to buy Thomas Hutchings's cotton factory on the Enoree River, 4 miles south of Pleasant Grove, when the county auctioned it in 1827. Three years later, as the factory prospered, Lester, desiring to move closer to that enterprise, offered the crossroads property for sale. Hugh Bailey, an Irish immigrant, bought the land.

Bailey took possession of Lester's plantation and continued farming and providing a rest stop for the countless drovers and drummers, agents, and adventurers continually passing. He acquired more land, extending his holdings

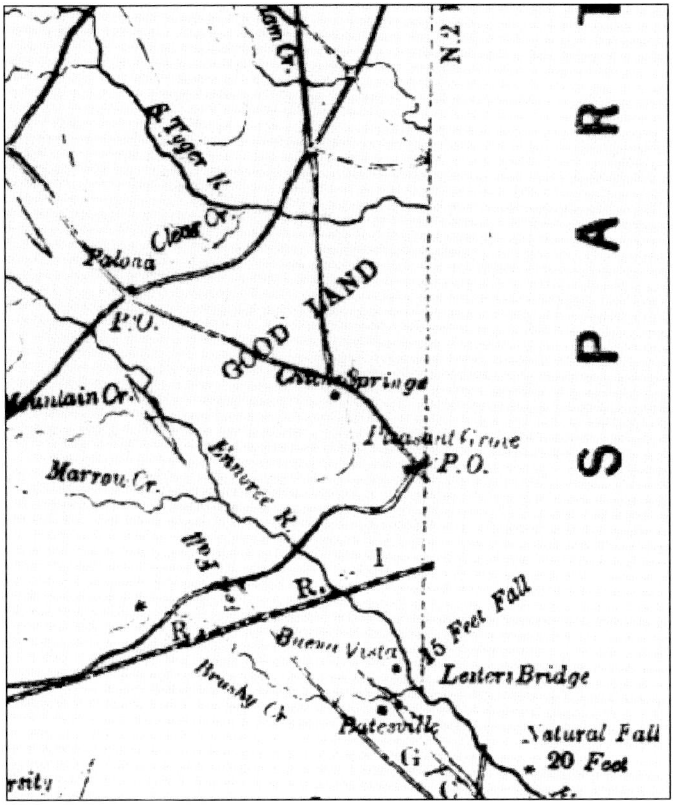


*GOOD LAND. An 1873 map of Greenville County suggests one motive for the rapid settlement of lands surrounding Greer. The land was classified as good for farming. Prices remained low because of relative isolation from the county seats of Greenville and Spartanburg.*

northward another mile. In 1834, he assumed the postmaster's position at Pleasant Grove and held it for two years until the post office was moved into Spartanburg County. From that time until the early twentieth century, when the community name reverted by custom back to Pleasant Grove, the settlement was known as Bailey's Crossroads.

The arrival of more settlers and land buyers in the area created a need for schools and churches. In 1833, a group of Baptists, in response to protracted effects from a revival that "broke out" at Brushy Creek Church in 1831 and was part of a national religious phenomenon known as the second "Great Awakening," organized Pleasant Grove Baptist Church. It was chartered under Act 2726 on December 20, 1837. Hugh Bailey had given the church its first property, a gift of a parcel of 1.6 acres deeded in 1833 that provided a permanent site for the meetinghouse and much of the cemetery. Presbyterians organized Mount Tabor nearby in 1841 and located it due south of the crossroads.

School at Bailey Crossroads consisted of informal tutoring by parents and occasionally by itinerant educators like Willis Threldkill, one of the first teachers in the area. Threldkill taught terms of varying lengths at several area communities, while adding to his teaching income by offering services as a Notary Public and land surveyor.

Upon his death in 1845, Bailey had amassed a significant estate of 20 slaves, land, and farm goods. His widow Elizabeth placed the estate, with the exception of almost 200 acres a mile north of the crossroads, in the hands of a widowed son-in-law. In 1844, another son-in-law, James T. Blakely, bought that piece of land and constructed a home close to the center of his property. Blakely farmed the land for almost two decades.

A future town located near the county line was much less certain before the Civil War and the arrival of a railroad, but considerable development of lands on and beyond the crossroads suggested potential commerce not strongly attached to either the Greenville or Spartanburg markets. During the antebellum era, three tiny cotton mills and a gold mine developed in an area of land a few miles wide that extended from the Enoree River north to the state line. Although two of the enterprises failed, the others attracted settlement and became central to the latter development of the town of Greer. Phillip Lester's cotton factory on the Enoree River prospered for three decades. The factory and lands were bought at auction in 1880, renamed Pelham Manufacturing Company, and operated for over 50 years. John Weaver and John Slack began operations of McCool's Shoals Factory as early as 1820. By the late 1820s, Weaver was sole owner of the mill located

*LINDSAY COLLINS. Confederate Veteran Lindsay Collins, shown with his wife, settled in the Double Springs Community after serving in the Confederate Army. The Double Springs area northwest of Greer developed as a farming community after the war.*

6 miles north of Pleasant Grove. Weaver's was a small spinning operation and, after surviving financial difficulties, continued to operate until Weaver's death in November 1862.

Thomas Hutchings, a minister from Rhode Island, was one of the founders of South Tyger Cotton Manufactory in 1833. Located 100 yards north of where Frohawk Creek joins the South Tyger River, about 2 miles from Bailey's Crossroads, the factory had been planned in 1833 and built some time afterward. By the early 1840s, the community surrounding the mill was known as Cedar Hill. The mill passed through the hands of many owners before 1876 when Isaac Lewis Green became majority owner. He, in turn, partnered with W.L. and A.J. Morgan, later with W.P. Taylor, separately with Nicholas Burgess, and upon that dissolution with L.A. Green. During the 1890s, the mill operated under the name of Arlington Factory and also as Arlington Cotton Mill. By 1902, Lewis Parker and Francis Pelzer had bought out the other stockholders and chartered Apalache Mill. The factory operated for almost 80 years.

Around the time Phillip Lester was ending his tenure as postmaster of Pleasant Grove, James H. Randolph discovered gold on his property about 8 miles to the north. He discovered gold in a quartz vein and worked it for a few months, but did not find a sufficient amount to warrant using his slaves for full-time mining. He sold the property to Vardry McBee, who worked the placer deposit with cheap white labor and slave labor until the beginning of the Civil War. McBee had better luck than did Randolph, the diggings producing close to $100,000 worth of gold, which McBee sold to the United States mint. In 1843, McBee gave interest in the gold mine to his daughter Martha and son-in-law Tench Carson. The mine became known thereafter as the Carson-McBee Mine. Carson died in 1861; McBee in 1864, leaving parts of the bottoms not worked. The gold was found in placer or alluvial deposits, having washed from eroded quartz veins called "stringers." Gold value amounted to between $10 and $32 worth per ton of ore. Even with the promise of gold—actually the certainty of it—McBee Bottoms remained un-worked for many years after his death. Still, the soil itself was valuable on two counts: excellent corn could be grown in the nutrient rich bottom land, and the red clay underlying the topsoil was of architectural quality. When the Biltmore House was constructed near Asheville, the fine-textured red clay of McBee Bottoms was used in creating some of the Biltmore tiling. The quality of the clay was such that samples were entered in the Nashville Exposition of 1895 by the Southern Railway and were awarded a competitive medal for quality.

# 2. RAILROAD TOWN: 1870S

While Bailey's Crossroads remained a rural community, the northern part of Hugh Bailey's estate became the epicenter of area growth and development. After farming his 190-acre tract for almost two decades, James T. Blakely sold the property in 1863 to W.F. Thackston for $4,000 in Confederate currency. James Manning Greer bought the land from Thackston and sold it to a Greenville investor in 1872, but not before he conveyed the right of way to the Atlanta & Richmond Airline Railroad. In an early census, Manning Greer, as he was known locally, was listed as a "bucker," a term used for men in the timber business who cut wood. Family tradition held that Greer swapped his land to the railroad for a team of mules and a wagon, but records indicate that he did have a cash agreement for the right of way, giving 100 feet on each side of the track for $5 and "benefits and advantages."

The proposed Airline Railroad would provide access to a vast inland area east from Atlanta across the Carolinas into Virginia. This land had great agricultural potential with the proper addition of guanos. On May 11, 1869, a public meeting at the Greenville Courthouse was held and a committee of five, consisting of William K. Easley, Henry P. Hammett, Benjamin Perry, Alexander McBee, and William T. Shumate, was appointed to work with officials of the railroad. By mid-1871, surveyors had selected a route that also ran through part of Alfred Taylor's land. Taylor, like Manning Greer, gave the railroad right of way across his land.

The individual who perhaps did everything necessary to establish Greer, except give it his name, was William Terry Shumate, a wounded veteran, former sheriff, businessman, and railroad speculator. Shumate believed a town would develop between Greenville and Spartanburg where the tracks intersected the old State Road and several country roads. After buying the land from Manning Greer, he hired surveyor H.P. Johnson to divide his tract into lots, ranging from a fraction of 1 acre to 40 acres, and then offered them to the public. The first transactions were made during late summer in 1873 by John W. Cunningham and William A. Hill, who promised to pay for lots on August 15, 1873; Cunningham agreeing to buy two and Hill one. Hill put down the first money, paying Shumate $5 down for a half-acre lot priced at $80. On September 13, Dr. Henry V. Westmoreland, a country doctor who had been in practice in the area since about 1870, made a down payment of $10 on one of Shumate's larger parcels. That same month, the Atlanta & Richmond Airline defaulted on its debt, one of the many reverses in railroading that created the economic panic of 1873. Suddenly, the future of the Shumate tract was in doubt. Neither Cunningham, Hill, nor Westmoreland completed their initial transactions.

The town envisioned by Shumate moved slightly closer toward reality when the first depot was completed by October 1873. The original structure housed both railway office and post office. William Clark Bailey, son of Hugh and Elizabeth Bailey, was the first depot agent assigned to the station. Designated by the Post Office Department as Greer's Depot, the future town consisted of a two-room depot and the house, barn, and outbuildings built by James Blakely. A loading platform had not been attached to the depot because, as a flag station, trains did not make regular stops. The little cargo arriving was off-loaded to the ground. Any passengers could have the station agent signal the train to stop in order to catch a ride to other points on the line.

Other than to cause some initial hesitancy, the nationwide depression of 1873 had minimal impact upon the birth and early years of Greer. The state's economy had been so miserably stagnant during Reconstruction that any business at all represented improvement, regardless of how slow it might develop. Prospects for a new town improved in 1874 when Shumate sold 9 of his 45 lots, comprising about one-fourth of the total acreage. William A. Hill was among those who bought in 1874, selecting the second-largest parcel in the survey. More important than Shumate's property transfers were those secondary deals involving others who had bought lots from him.

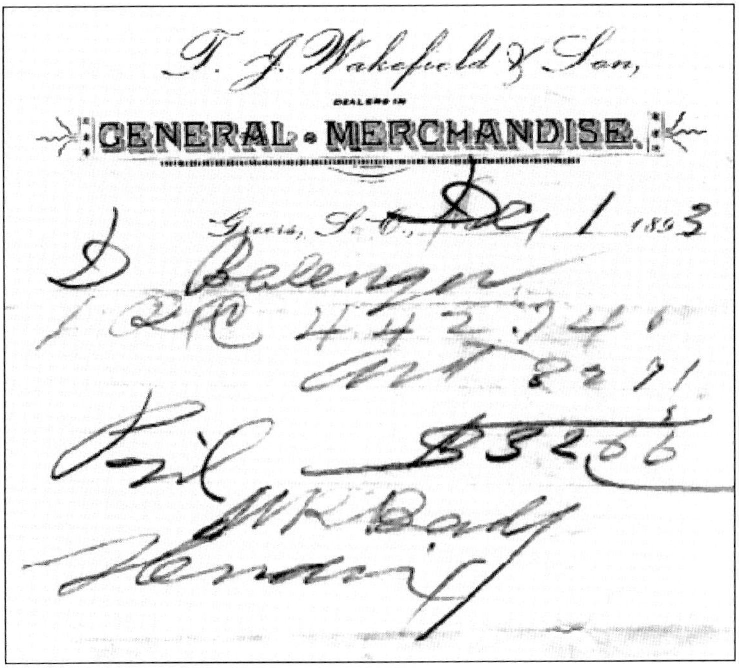
T. J. Wakefield & Son,
DEALERS IN
GENERAL • MERCHANDISE.

*WAKEFIELD GENERAL MERCHANDISE. Greers, as it was known well into the twentieth century, offered plenty of business for general merchants like T.J. Wakefield's store. Virtually every general merchant accepted cotton in lieu of cash from area farmers.*

Land speculation fueled interest in Greer's Depot, created something of a real estate boom before 1880, and attracted permanent settlers. On March 25, 1876, by Act No. 183 of the South Carolina Legislature, Greer became a town. While the first post office was called "Greer's Depot," the people (all 15 of them) voted to incorporate and drop "Depot" from the name. The act stated that the "town shall be called and known by the name of Greer's, and its limits shall be deemed and held to extend one-half a mile in each direction from the Air Line Railroad Depot at said place." Locals often called it Greer's Station and that name, as well as Greer's Depot, continued to appear in local church records and newspapers for some years. By the time schoolteacher Miss Anna Greene wrote her *Short Sketch of the Town of Greers, S.C.* in 1896, the apostrophe had disappeared. The official charter from the Secretary of State on February 11, 1905 listed the name as the town of Greers. In 1901, the post office dropped the "s," but the town continued to be called Greers well into the 1920s.

By 1879, Greer's boasted 250 inhabitants, a school, and 4 stores that, according to the *Greenville Enterprise and Mountaineer*, did "considerable trade." The earliest stores in town all sold whiskey, creating an initial reputation for Greer as a place unfit for ladies to walk on its streets. An innovation of the Airline Railroad did nothing to relieve Greer of its reputation as a rough and open town. The refrigerator car was a relatively new addition to railroad service when the Airline Railroad had one built and placed on the rails by late summer 1879; the technology had been in existence only about four years and was virtually unknown in the South. Painted white and decorated with grotesquely crafted figures, it became known to train watchers and the thirsty as the "circus car." It brought refreshment to towns along the line in the form of freshly brewed beer from Atlanta breweries.

The town charter contained a provision for the town council to appoint marshals and constables as needed; however, long before town officers were employed, laws were enforced and order kept by mutual consent of citizens and by constables serving under area trial justices. During its early years, the greatest challenges to public order in Greer were rowdy drunks. Determined to eliminate this problem, citizens petitioned the state legislature to make Greer a dry town. The legislature acted on the request on December 11, 1879, prohibiting the sale of spirits within Greer and 2 miles of its corporate limits.

As chief executive officer, the mayor was ultimately responsible for enforcing the law. On September 2, 1880, horse thief Tilman Acree escaped from the Greenville County jail at 7:30 p.m. and headed for parts unknown. Towns along the telegraph lines were advised to be on the lookout. At 2:40 p.m. the next day, Mayor William A. Hill telegraphed the sheriff to come and get Acree, who had been identified and captured at Greer.

In 1881, Act 452 of the state legislature created a trial justice position for Greer with special jurisdiction in both Greenville and Spartanburg Counties. This authority included the right of the trial justice to appoint constables as needed. Thaddeus T. Westmoreland was appointed to this position.

*OLD LETTER, 1893. A letter from T.E. Smith to his brother bears the old postmark "Greers Depot."*

Since Greer was now a dry town by law, the whiskey trade ceased on the street, but continued in the shadows. Long established in the country and mountains, the trade in spirits was considered a legitimate and often necessary business. Mountain farmers compensated for their smaller crops per acre by turning some of their grain into spirits. Local trade in the product continued as the store buildings went up. In-migration also brought families to town, a majority of whom opposed the whiskey trade not only as a public enterprise, but on the principle that it posed an ever-present threat to public morality.

Without regular officers on duty, the town's liquor law was virtually unenforceable. Greer's Depot was not only a destination for moonshiners, but was located on the crossroads of the trade carried to nearby towns and villages. Cider and whiskey from the Dark Corner, the upper part of the county, traveled in wagons laden with produce and cotton as farmers made their way to Greer to trade and to get their cotton ginned and sold. While law enforcement was unable to make many inroads against this type of offense, a united effort by the community to control the whiskey traffic came to Greer in the form of a chapter of the Independent Order of Good Templars. The Templars, a national prohibition and temperance organization, arrived in South Carolina and, by 1872, had spread over the state. At least one chapter of Templars was organized within 3 miles of Greer by 1878. The local lodge No. 128 was likely organized in 1881 in reaction to the still bothersome whiskey trade.

Pierce Thompson, lodge deputy, led the local Templars. W.A. Hill provided a meeting place for Greer Templars over his general store. Through educational speeches, public plays, preaching, and person-to-person encounters, the Greer

Templars were initially effective in ridding the town of the alcohol nuisance. By March 1881, the *Greenville Enterprise and Mountaineer* bragged of Greer, "It is not within the command of language for a stronger plea to be made for the total abolition of the sale of whiskey in South Carolina than the recital of the recent history of our little neighbor." Six months later, the same newspaper reported, "Greer folks are naturally clever, anyhow, and all the Good Templars felt perfectly at home, knowing how to appreciate Temperance, having benefited so much by prohibition in the once disturbed but now quiet and thriving little town." Influence of the Templars worked for years. It was reported in 1884 that Greer had no need for either police or a guardhouse.

The Templars of Greer reorganized on August 11, 1883. J. Harrison Boyd, M.B. Cunningham, Noah Cannon, and Ida Dickson formed the core leadership. The new Greer organization, the Airline Lodge 187, hosted the county meeting on July 15, 1885. Election of officers was held on August 1; officers included M.F. Dillard, Bertha Carman, Fannie Cannon, W.P. and Sallie Few, Ida Goodlett, I.L. Green, Dr. Benjamin F. Few, R.L. Green, Ila Dillard, J.B. Garron, J.T. Taylor (probably J.P. Taylor), G.V. Bell, J.L. Carman, and Reverend W.S. Martin. An area convention of Good Templars met at Chick Springs on August 27, 1885; Reverend W.S. Martin was speaker. By mid-1886, the local lodge had 60 members, but the movement had less interest elsewhere in the county. Greer's Templars presented the well-worn temperance play *Ten Nights in a Bar Room* on December 27, 1887. Money collected was to benefit the Baptist church.

Perhaps the crucial factor in the decline of the Templars in the late 1880s was a perceived threat to the unity of the Democratic Party. Party leaders discouraged the continuation of temperance as a "movement" by 1886 because it, like the Greenback Party and the Patrons of Husbandry, held potential to "ruin the Democratic Party." Another factor in the decline of the Templars may have had to do with the composition of the organization. While it had had powerful moral force, its political power did not reflect the strength of its numbers, many of whom were non-voting females. The argument, which centered upon "Democratic ruin," may have appealed more to those who actually voted. The declining interest in the Templar movement may also have reflected willingness to accept regulation of liquor as a reasonable achievement. Despite the decline of the Templars as an organization, Greer remained adamantly opposed to liquor. An election was held in Greenville County on March 14, 1888 to decide the question of licensing liquor dealers. County-wide, licensing won by a majority of 154 votes; the local vote at Greer's Depot opposed licensing by a tally of 30 for and 90 against.

Once law and moral pressure set the tone in Greer, its growing citizenry got down to the business of building and rebuilding lives. In 1880, the Airline Railroad itself gave the town a boost when it employed an itinerant land agent to promote the development of the tiny towns growing up along the tracks. The land agent promoted sale of lands near the depots and provided information about available farmland and soil fertility. After the arrival of churches and a school, Greer attracted earnest businessmen and young men, who were less transient and more interested in the long-term prospects of the town. Some newcomers were branching out in their already successful businesses elsewhere, notably H.C. Mark of Greenville. Others, such as brothers Thaddeus and H.V Westmoreland and W.A. Hill, had arrived as experienced businessmen from other locations to set up anew. Many young men, like Olin Gaines and John Robinson, were in transition from farm to city to find and seize opportunity.

Gaines, who came to Greer as a young telegraph operator, went to work for the railroad in 1881 at the age of 14. As he gained seniority, he became entrenched in local business and society. He worked for the railroad until he was in his mid-30s. By then, Greer had more than doubled in population and business volume. Gaines married the daughter of Noah Cannon, a prominent farmer, who was a founder of Victor Cotton Manufacturing Company. After Gaines left the railroad to work in the mill office, he rose to general manager of accounting by 1915.

William C. Bailey remained depot agent until his death in 1882. W.A. Pollard of Fountain Inn succeeded Bailey, but left in 1884 to become the postmaster. D.T. Lane, who replaced Pollard, served four years until 18-year-old John A. Robinson succeeded him in October 1888. Robinson, a Spartanburg County farm boy, grew up with the town and became an instrument of its progress. In his early 30s, he was associated with Lewis Parker when Parker was president of Victor Manufacturing

*JOHN ROBINSON'S HOME. Robinson's early 1900s brick home was, like his neighbors' in early Greer, suggestive of the kind of success possible in a New South cotton town when one applied hard work and diligence to his labors.*

*JOHN ROBINSON AS A YOUNG MAN. John Robinson arrived in Greer as a telegraph clerk for the railroad from the Cashville community in Spartanburg County.*

Company and making plans for the construction of Apalache. Robinson went on to found Greer Manufacturing Company in 1909 and move into other business ventures and civic involvement during the remaining 76 years of his life. Other young men, like Burgess brothers William and Frank, began their professional lives not far from the farm, in the cotton trade, but recognized opportunity and permitted their interests to evolve with business trends to cotton manufacturing and related interests that extended far beyond Greer.

After the economic depression of the 1870s ended, railroad business across the country had caught up with railroad mileage. The Airline's single track had to accommodate more trains as business between towns on the line increased. Spurs and sidetracks allowed passage of trains, moving in opposite directions, to move mail, passengers, and freight.

If the coming of the railroad was solely responsible for the founding of Greer, then the debt owed the railroad was amply repaid by the commerce that passed from the countryside through Greer into the mainstream of business. The first freight shipped to Greer over the Airline was a consignment of fertilizer, pitched off on the side of the tracks where consignees Dr. Henry V. Westmoreland, John

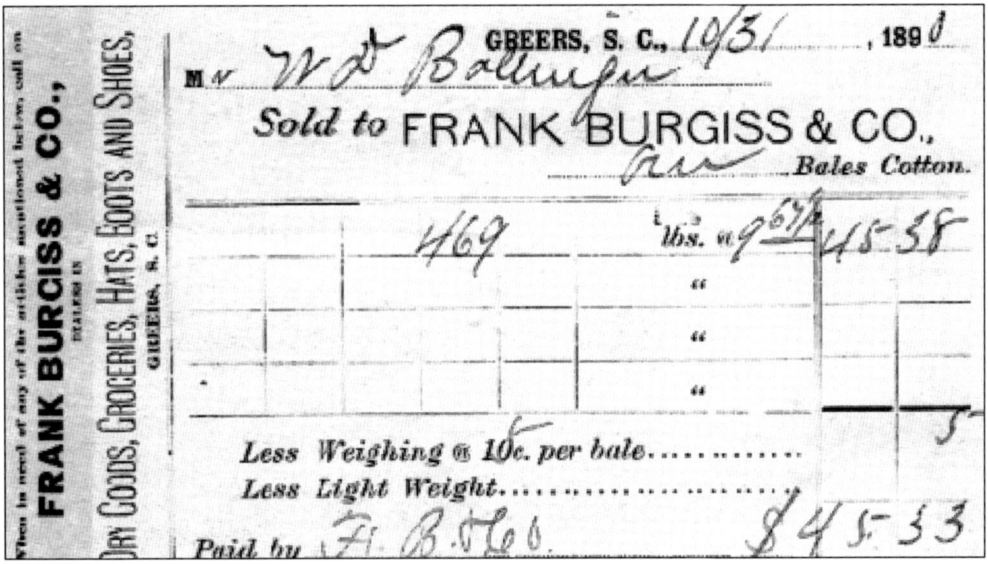
FRANK BURGISS & CO.,
DEALERS IN
DRY GOODS, GROCERIES, HATS, BOOTS AND SHOES,
GREERS, S. C.
GREERS, S. C., 189
M
Sold to FRANK BURGISS & CO.,
Bales Cotton.
lbs. @
Less Weighing @ 10c. per bale............
Less Light Weight......................
Paid by

*FRANK BURGESS, COTTON BUYER. Frank Burgess founded the cotton market in Greer. Shipping by rail made Burgess's business a success. By the 1890s, he was a specialist in long staple cotton and a buying agent for Clifton Mills.*

W. Cunningham, and J.M. Littlefield claimed it. The use of commercial fertilizers and guanos was something of a novelty in the upstate after the Civil War.

Cotton, during the waning months of the war, had soared to nearly $2 per pound. In the Piedmont and mountains, however, with less cotton produced, some small farmers based their cashless economy on grain. Pettice Prince, an illiterate white farm laborer, agreed in January 1871 to work for David Cannon for 12 months "to the best of his skill and ability" in return for six and a half bushels of corn per month to be paid in November at harvest. Many local farmers were subsistence farmers, who made little more than a living, but were freeholders of land and relatively independent. The promotion of cotton as a cash crop and the use of commercial supplements to grow it changed the nature of farming after 1880. Cotton prices were down considerably from the heady market at war's end, but still at a level that offered farmers a chance for prosperity, especially if they also invested in guano. Cotton agriculture created the first prosperity in Greer and assured the new town of commerce.

William A. Hill, the first established fertilizer agent in Greer, shipped in supplies for his general store. General merchants, who followed him into business in Greer, also found that it paid handsomely to become agents for one or more guano manufacturers in Charleston or Savannah. Noah Cannon, for example, an early local dealer in fertilizer, sold one of the highest grades of fertilizer in the state. By April 1882, Simeon Hughes, who had already moved 200 tons of fertilizer, expected to sell another 30 tons while cotton planting was underway. In less than a decade after Hill came to town, a dozen guano dealers were in business.

Regardless of the station of farmer—whether landlord, tenant, or cropper—guano had to be bought and, most often, bought on credit. Bad crop years meant deeper extension into debt, but good years did not necessarily mean debt freedom. Bad years meant greater purchase of fertilizers, if anything, in anticipation of a bumper crop of cotton, which would allow the farmer to reduce his debt or once again be free of a lien holder. For the railroad, bad years for the farmers meant guaranteed fertilizer shipments for the next season. Good years for farmers with large cotton crops also meant heavy business for the railroad. The central location of Greer, almost equidistant from Greenville and Spartanburg, created a local cotton business by 1882 that developed, in time, into a fairly sophisticated cotton market, seriously competitive with Greenville and Spartanburg for farmers' business.

Between 1896 and 1909, three cotton mills were constructed at Greer: Victor, Franklin, and Greer Manufacturing Company. Apalache was built a mile from town in 1902. Pelham and the small operation at Cedar Hill had received and shipped freight other than raw cotton or fertilizers since 1880 or earlier. With the arrival of modern mills, additional cotton was brought to local mills and the finished cloth and yarn shipped to markets. Along with freight, increased passenger traffic reflected the arrival of mill hands, who would remain as permanent residents, and the arrival and departure of increasing numbers of visitors, salesmen, and opportunists.

As freight increased and the number of trains correspondingly so, the railroad brought with it the realities of any technological innovation, including the potential for tragedy. Accidents involving the trains and pedestrians, trains and mule-drawn wagons, and trains and natural disasters occurred. One of the earliest recorded train accidents occurred in 1883. Edward McKittrick was killed while walking the tracks from Greenville to his home near Greer. In another accident, John Martin, a freight brakeman, slipped and fell between cars and was killed just outside the city limits in September 1899. In winter 1903, a 16-year-old African American, Henry Rudolph, was killed when struck by No. 97, a fast mail train.

Greer's worst railroad accident occurred in 1887 when a head-on collision of two trains occurred near the cut west of Greer at Buncombe Road. On October 20, passenger train 51 with nine cars received permission to run four hours and twenty minutes behind schedule. It carried a number of passengers back to the upstate from the Atlanta Exposition and approached Greer from the west at 5:40 a.m. Stations along the Airline had been notified by telegraph that train 51 had the right of way. At about the same time, engineer Joe Harris pulled his special freight train out of Greer's Depot. Harris knew about train 51, but calculated that he had time to reach a sidetrack down the line at Taylors' Station where train 51 would make a safe pass.

Since the grade was a decline to Taylors; the heavier freight train was probably traveling in excess of 30 miles per hour when it reached the cut at Buncombe Road. Overcast skies and drizzle obscured visibility for engineers of both trains. By the time the lights of each could be seen from the other, it was impossible

The Greer Observer.

VOL. II. NO. 29. GREER, S. C., THURSDAY, JANUARY 17, 1907. $1.00 PER YEAR

DR. BENNETT DEAD

GREER OBSERVER. *The* Greer Observer *was Greer's first newspaper, beginning publication in 1905.*

to avoid collision. Both engines were destroyed, the explosion of the boilers scattering metal over hundreds of yards. Most of the cars derailed and the first three cars of the freight train caught fire. Engineer Robert Wall of train 51 and Mrs. Hampton McDowell were killed in the wreck; a dozen more were injured. Fireman G.L. Webster of the freight train, badly scalded and with one arm hideously dislocated, somehow managed to walk to Greer's Depot where he gave the alarm. Webster was treated and later sent to Spartanburg for better care where he died that evening of his injuries.

A special train carrying doctors was sent from Greenville to transport the injured back to the Greenville Exchange Hotel, which served as a hospital. Greer had no facilities to deal with an emergency of that scale. Trial Justice Thaddeus T. Westmoreland held an inquest later in the day and determined that Joe Harris and conductor John Reville were responsible. Harris and Reville had left the scene before they were questioned; the inquest was held in their absence. Joe Harris surrendered to Sheriff Gilreath on November 1 and was charged with murder. It became clear after investigation that Harris's inexperience and unclear railroad policy, rather than recklessness, had caused the accident. He was not prosecuted.

In 1894, the Airline became known as the Southern Railway after some years of financial troubles, mergers, and reorganizations. Its commercial growth continued, stimulated by the growth of towns and the building of cotton mills.

Natural disasters also took a toll on early railroad construction. The freshet of 1903 destroyed or damaged every bridge, including railway trestles in the Greer area, holding up rail traffic three days. Floods in 1908 washed out an embankment 85 feet long and 50 feet high. By then, construction techniques had advanced to the degree that the track was re-laid just days after a crew constructed a trestle of the same dimensions.

By the turn of the century, eight or more scheduled freight, passenger, and mail trains per day passed through Greer, as well as special express trains and frequent excursion trains to larger towns on the line. The rise of cotton mills in towns along the Airline brought an increase in passenger traffic. Greer's growth also mandated more control over the vehicles passing through the town. Automobile speeds were regulated and, in 1905, the town council passed an ordinance prohibiting train speeds in excess of 15 miles per hour.

By 1907, Greer had outgrown its first depot. The *Greer Observer*, impatient with the company, suggested editorially that the Public Improvement Committee of the Board of Trade take the matter to the Railroad Commission. Commissioners visited Greer to examine the depot, but no commitment was immediately made. By 1909, the railroad business was so heavy that spurs and sidetracks no longer sufficed to control the rail traffic. The section of the Southern Line between Greenville and Spartanburg was double-tracked. Construction on a new depot was finally scheduled to begin on May 15, 1909. The new "large commodious" depot was completed in early 1910.

VICTOR MANUFACTURING. *Organized in 1895 and funded almost entirely by Greer investors, the mill was made profitable by second president Lewis Parker, who bought controlling interest and eventually created the state's first textile conglomerate, Parker Mills.*

# 3. GROWING PAINS: 1880–1900

By 1891, businesses had more than doubled to 11 merchants, although the resident population was still only 300. Greer grew slowly until the founding of Victor Manufacturing Company in 1895. By 1898, the population stood at 1,200 and the commercial population expanded as well. Seven years later, Greer claimed 39 merchants (14 of whom owned general stores), a bank, two smithies, and a total financial strength, including the corporate finances of two cotton mills (Franklin had been built in 1900) of $574,000. The *Greenville Daily News*, in 1906, described Greer as "thriving." Two years later, Greer was designated a "city" in an article appearing in the *Greenville Daily News*.

Although commerce and economic advantage motivated the settlement, advancement in other ways besides commerce was necessary to insure viability. Religious faith and education were promoted with such zeal that it helped to unify immediate residents of Greer with country and crossroads citizens, adding an important dimension to how area folk perceived themselves and their affiliations then and later.

W.T. Shumate offered lots to congregations of Methodists, Baptists, and Presbyterians who would build churches in Greer. The Presbyterians of Mount Tabor, located at Bailey's Crossroads, were the first to take advantage of the offer, receiving title to a lot on November 16, 1880. The church building was moved from its original site at Bailey's Crossroads by using mules and cables to pull the building as it rolled on logs.

By May 1881, Mount Tabor's congregation built a new frame house of worship. The Reverend Robert H. Reid, with the Reverend C.B. Stewart participating, preached the dedication service held on May 28. The 1,800-square-foot structure was estimated to have cost (including bell and a fresh coat of paint) about $1 per square foot. The old church building remained on the lot until after 1922 and was gone by 1930. Presbyterians or other denominations may have met in the old building long before Mount Tabor was organized in 1841. In 1919, it was estimated to be more than 100 years old.

The Baptists took possession of their lot and constructed a meetinghouse, which was demolished by a summer storm on August 10, 1881. The church had been used for only two services when the storm flattened it. Trees were uprooted

*VICTOR MANUFACTURING. Shortly after the turn of the century, Victor Cotton Manufacturing Company had become known as one of the model mills in the state. It provided housing, churches, a school, and a store for workers.*

and damage was done to other buildings nearby, but there was no loss of life. Within a week, the wreckage had been cleared and the lot readied for rebuilding. While the Baptists were having their own difficulties, the Presbyterians shared with them their meeting space. Sugar James was in charge of construction on the new Baptist building. It was slow work because the small congregation had little in the way of funds. First services were conducted in the second meetinghouse on November 5, 1882.

The churches of Greer were tiny at first, as was the population of the town. In order to fill up the pews, the churches agreed on a schedule to hold the town's preaching service in the Baptist building on the first Sunday, in the Presbyterian church on the second and fourth Sundays, and at the Methodist meeting place on the third Sunday. Sunday school was held in the Presbyterian church every Sunday since William C. Bailey had organized a Union Sunday School for all denominations.

Although the Methodists had not yet constructed a church by October 1884, they had built a nice parsonage for their minister, the Reverend L.F. Beatty. It was a painted, two-story structure with a tin roof. The previous minister, the Reverend J.L. Tilman, had provided his own housing at Greer in 1881. Before they constructed a church, the Methodists met at different locations, including the Presbyterian church and in spacious upstairs "halls" over general stores such as Hezekiah Moore's and W.A. Hill's. In May 1886, the congregation was in the hall over Moore's store since he had promised them free use until the fall of the year.

*FIRST BAPTIST CHURCH, SECOND BUILDING. The First Baptist church was originally located on Cannon Avenue. The first structure was destroyed by a storm in 1880. This illustration shows the second structure on the same site, completed by 1881.*

The earliest African-American Baptist church outlying Greer was New Shady Grove at Reidville, presided over by Reverend S.L. Foster. In 1873, its seven members belonged to the Enoree Association. Piney Grove Baptist, a mile north of Zoar in Spartanburg County, was organized in 1879 and also presided over by Reverend Foster. Black churches developed more slowly and later than did the new white churches of Greer because they had fewer members concentrated near town to carry on the organizational and building work. For a long time, meetings were held in individual homes as small congregations had little money for construction.

Two other African-American congregations, Mount Lebanon Baptist and Zion Hill, both led by Reverend S.B. McGhee, met at Greer; the first was active between 1886 and 1893 with between 20 and 40 members and the second apparently organized around 1890. Zion Hill reported 25 baptisms and 61 members in 1890, plus membership in the Enoree River Association. Reverend McGhee was apparently a circuit rider and church organizer, attending to several churches on a rotating basis, which was true of his white Baptist counterparts in the early days of Greer. By 1894, Reverend McGhee was doing organizational work in Duncan.

The earliest recorded African-American church within Greer was Bethel Methodist Episcopal Church, which was organized by Reverend Benjamin Robinson and several families (Butler, Greer, Mayfield, and Davis) in 1882. The church held its first meetings in private homes until trustees Adam Mayfield,

Pickens Butler, Ansel Johnson, and James Greer bought a lot in January 1888, in what was then part of Spartanburg County, for the purpose of constructing a church. Date of construction of the first meetinghouse has not been determined, but a new house of worship was built in 1921 at a cost of $10,000. Members of the church, who were skilled carpenters or other craftsmen, constructed the second church building.

St. Marcus African Methodist Episcopal Church was also an early black church in Greer. Members bought a lot and scheduled the dedication of the church for February 10, 1884. Located on the site of the present-day Maple Creek Baptist Church property, the members of St. Marcus mortgaged the church property four years later to Allen and Welborn Gosnell, sawyers and lumber dealers. The note could not be paid and the Gosnells foreclosed in 1891 without recovery.

*FIRST BAPTIST CHURCH, SECOND LOCATION. The First Baptist Church outgrew its original location and was moved twice more. The second location was the east side of Poinsett Street shown here.*

Meanwhile, Maple Creek Baptist Church had been organized and members were meeting in the storeroom of merchant Noah Cannon. When the St. Marcus property became available, trustees James Priestly and J.E. Washington signed a promissory note on behalf of Maple Creek to the Gosnells and Noah Cannon, who also owned land adjacent to the church property, guaranteeing payment. The price of the land, including the old church building, was $365. For years, the congregation was unable to pay much on the debt. If Cannon retained interest in the property, it was never recorded. In 1907, when Maple Creek found itself in a position to pay off its outstanding notes, the Gosnells charged no interest for the lapse and Noah Cannon, who had forgotten the exact date he had guaranteed the debt, sold any remaining interest in the land for $5.

The churches of Greer struggled to build both membership and houses of worship during the early years of the town. By the end of 1887, congregations of Greer, black and white, were involved in fundraising. Prospects of fellowship and entertainment encouraged the public to attend. The Methodists, who continued to use W.A. Hill's guano storeroom, held a supper and raised $90. A temperance play performed at the high school brought in $150 for the Baptists, while the Maple Creek Baptists held a supper at Noah Cannon's store and raised $20.

While the citizens of Greer built their houses of worship, they also built their schools. Tradition says that David Cannon agreed to buy a lot and move to Greer if others would join him and build a school. He bought 30 acres from William T. Shumate in 1874 and, after the last of his cotton was picked, he packed his belongings and moved his family to Greer on February 27, 1875. William A. Hill, one of the earliest merchants of Greer, furnished a log cabin on the northeast corner at the intersection of Mosteller (Main Street) and Hill Streets (East Poinsett Street). The cabin was heated by a low, flat cordwood stove. Rough lumber planks, placed on square chestnut blocks, were arranged around the stove for sitting with the children facing inward. They studied the fundamentals of reading, writing, and arithmetic; grammar was added to the curriculum later. The length of the public school term varied with the funds available to pay teachers, but averaged three months in the winter and six weeks in summer. When the cabin school outgrew its building, W.A. Hill again provided a place in a room over his cotton gin house. The *Greenville Enterprise and Mountaineer* reported, on July 30, 1879, that school was about the only thing citizens of Greer could agree upon. Since the cabin school was in need of repair, a building committee was appointed, but was blocked from proceeding with plans by court order.

Sallie Cannon of Spartanburg County, 22 years old, was the first teacher at the Greer's school. After passing her county teacher's exam on January 14, 1875, she opened her school in Greer sometime after February 27, 1875, possibly during the lay-by of the cotton crop in mid-summer. The first school in Greer was open to the public and received state funding through the county board. In 1877, brother and sister Horace and Carrie King succeeded Sallie Cannon, who continued teaching in Spartanburg County. After the Kings, N.K. Vance and Charles Key

*MOSTELLER MILL. Constructed in 1814, Mosteller Mill was the earliest grist mill in the Greer area. Located north of Greer on South Tyger River, it operated for over 150 years and at various times served as a community gathering spot, post office, and a trial justice court. Mosteller Road, the road to the mill, became Mosteller Street at Greer's town limits. By the early twentieth century, Mosteller Street was known as Greer's main street.*

taught short sessions. Other early short-term teachers were John Edens and Edward Dawson, who served as co-principals.

Of these earliest teachers, Sallie Dorrah had the most longevity, returning for sessions from 1878 through 1881. Since sessions were short, she divided her time between Greer and Greenville. Daughter of Greenville physician J.F. Dorrah, she received her first grade certificate on June 28, 1873, while living in the Fairview community near Fountain Inn. She was a prime example of the "new woman" of the post-bellum South. Arriving in a rough and ready railroad town where the barrooms and their rough patrons made the safety of the streets uncertain, Sallie Dorrah nevertheless left the security and certainty of her parents' home to pursue a profession. After a year, she moved her school in 1879 from Hill's cotton gin house to a spare room located across the street on the southeast corner of the intersection. Once more, she moved to the Masonic Hall, located in the middle of the 200th block of Trade Street.

After six years and several unsatisfactory school locations, interest in education was sufficiently high that, in 1880, citizens formed a joint stock company to build an adequate school. The Greer Educational Association sold stock at the rate of $20 per share, members being permitted to hold only one share, although additional contributions could be made. A board of trustees consisted of six men: two Baptists, two Methodists, and two Presbyterians. The first board consisted of W.E. Carver, John Landrum Carman, A.A. Dempsey, Cunningham Pennington, J.H. Boyd, and John M. Dickson. Within a year, the association had 30 members. Students were charged $1 per term for tuition.

Murray B. Manly, son of Dr. Basil Manly, former chaplain of the Confederacy, was hired as the first principal of the school. Sallie Dorrah, who had managed alone for three years, assisted him. The first order of business for the association was construction of a new building, completed by March 1881. The frame building, measuring 24 by 48 feet, with a bell cupola, was located adjacent to the Presbyterian church on a lot provided by W.T. Shumate at nominal cost.

Joseph Whitener Kennedy, who had previously headed the school at Fairview near Fountain Inn, succeeded Manly as principal in 1881. Kennedy had completed only two years of college before arriving at the age of 27. By early November 1881, Professor Kennedy opened the Greer's High School, a tuition school. The lower grades were funded by county taxes and free to the public; students in the upper grades were charged tuition. His classes numbered about 60 pupils. The school became a drawing card for the new town as Kennedy promoted his school in newspaper advertisements and through word of mouth. The school's superior offerings, which included double entry bookkeeping, music, and oil painting, were available to members of both sexes. At the end of the session, Sallie Dorrah returned to teach in Greenville.

During the spring session of 1882, Professor Kennedy and one assistant opened the school at the elementary, primary, and academic levels for a modest rate of $5, $7.50, and $10, respectively, per five-month session. While free school continued to be available, the session was short. Students desiring a full year of education were willing to pay tuition. Demand for quality education brought in students from the outlying communities. Students from just a few miles distant in any direction required some sort of housing for the sake of convenience, and local residents found opportunity in offering room and board to scholars for the going rate of $10 per month. For the fall session, 13 students from a distance sufficient to require boarding facilities had applied.

Kennedy's school was enthusiastically received. Dr. Benjamin F. Few was among a number of country citizens who were able to move to Greer solely for the benefit of their children, that they might attend school at Greer. Few's family arrived in Greer in time to enroll his children in the school for the fall term, having turned over his practice at Sandy Flat to Dr. W.T. Stoddard, formerly of Greer. T. Whitner McDowell of Fairview moved to Greer for the "superior advantages offered by our high school." Greer's High School quickly became a major attraction for the community. P.A.H. Jenkins, who moved from Reidville to Greer to enroll his three sons in the school, rented his farm in order to make the move. Alda Patterson, age eight, wrote to Uncle Arch of the *Greenville Enterprise and Mountaineer* on May 5, 1885, describing Kennedy's school as "splendid."

In fall 1882, Kennedy was elected to the school commission and established his office in the old location of the county supervisor of registration office. He continued to operate the school in Greer while serving in his new capacity, employing John Manley and J.T. Woodside to preside at the school while he performed his county duties. Visiting the country schools often, he made recommendations based upon first-hand observations and raised the level of professionalism of the office of superintendent. Kennedy was the first Greenville County School Commissioner to make an official written report in 1883.

Growth of Greer prompted the county to divide the district into two parts. During Reconstruction, the county was subdivided into townships for administrative purposes; each township became a school district until population increase required further subdivision. In 1883, District Nine, Chick Springs Township, was subdivided; the eastern portion containing Greer was designated as District 18, East Chick Springs District. A new public school was established for Greer-area students in 1885. This one-room school was located on Mosteller Road (Highway 14). The trustees of the new district, Dr. Henry V. Westmoreland, Simeon Hughes, and J.P. Smith, bought property on Mosteller Road from Isaac Wright and Robert Gray.

Kennedy accepted a job at Fairview Township and was succeeded in the fall term of 1886 by Reverend J.R. Plyler, who was assisted by his wife. While the school offered levels of instruction, it was not truly a graded school with separate classrooms for each grade level. The state legislature created Greers Graded School District on December 24, 1887. Its boundaries included all area within a half-mile radius of Greer's Academy. When the district was created, the town had to decide whether to build a new school or to add to the academy built by the Greer's Educational Association. Either way, all public school funds for 1888 were committed to the building fund and no free public school was held at Greer that calendar year. Classes were held only at the private school for paying scholars. The graded school plan excited more interest among those seeking educational opportunities for their children. In January 1888, the housing shortage was exacerbated. All available building lots had been sold. The *Greenville Enterprise and Mountaineer* estimated that if housing was available, Greer's population would increase by 25 percent just on the basis of the education it afforded residents.

Professor James A. Dodd of Campobello became the principal of the high school on January 1, 1888. An experienced teacher, he specialized in English and the classical languages. In August, the Greer's Educational Association turned over the property to the Graded School trustees, who decided to add two rooms to the existing structure. Sliding partitions were built so the school could be converted to one large room for meetings. Fifty-five subscribers pledged to help pay for the work. By September 1889, 41 had paid their pledges and trustees bought new school furniture through W.J. Thackston, the purchase consisting of 30 to 40 pieces to be delivered in time for the fall term.

William D. McCorkle, a Washington & Lee graduate, and J.H. Nolan, South Carolina Military Academy graduate, opened the high school in fall 1888 with 60 pupils. Free school funds provided only a two-month term of public education in 1891. When the school opened in September 1893, R.H. Griffith served as principal, assisted by Mamie Folger. Tuition rates ranged from $1 to $3 for the session. In 1894, Superintendent W.E. Dendy and his assistant Lou Tindall directed school. During his second and third terms, Mamie Wells, Anna Green, Alta Patterson, and music teacher Marie Meacham assisted him.

M.H. Daniel of Spartanburg, assisted by Maggie Wells and Anna Green, served until 1898. The next year, Principal D. Belharri Simpson taught with Maggie Wells, Lucy Watson, and Miss Olive Bennett. Simpson was former principal of the female high school at Reidville. In 1898, there were 110 students enrolled in the "pay school," which set forth its objectives in *The Catalogue of Greers High School*:

> . . . give boys and girls a thorough training in the Common and high school branches of learning, and developed them morally and mentally that they may make useful and patriotic citizens. The school makes a specialty in preparing boys and girls for college.

The Greer's High School consisted of eight grades, which students were advised could be accomplished one per year with proper diligence and punctual attendance. President B.F. Wilson of Converse College gave a scholarship to Greer High to take effect in 1898. The recipient was determined by success on a competitive exam given by the principal and a scholarship committee.

The tuition school at Greer only met the needs of a portion of the children. While the pay school attracted students from financially secure families, the free public school classes operated only three months in 1899. By the turn of the century, Victor Manufacturing Company provided an elementary school for the workers' children, an education superior to that of the public education offered by the town itself. The mill school operated for 10 months and had 98 pupils, many of whom were attending school for the first time.

The history of African-American education in the area is sketchy. Some record of black teachers exists in lists of teacher examinees. Two African-American teachers who lived in the Buena Vista (Pelham) community, Alfred Raines and George Sloan, were certified by examination on January 1, 1879 and January 1, 1889, respectively. Sallie Watts, who took the exam on January 1, 1880, was issued a first grade certificate; she lived in Sandy Flat. The first black teacher who was living in Greer when he received certification was R.L. Garlington. A Greenville newspaper reported early in 1884 that "the colored children, as well as the white ones are going to school generally."

The locations of most other early African-American schools are unknown. Perhaps they were in the vicinity of black churches, which, by the turn of the century, had become strong enough to sponsor local private schools. The trustees of Jubilee Colored Church gave the O'Neal School District a lot for a colored free school in November 1897. The trustees of the Colored Methodist Church (Bethel) leased a building on church property to the black chapter of the Grand

*VICTOR VILLAGE ELEMENTARY SCHOOL. Victor Elementary School was built on company property by Victor Manufacturing Company. The building, very modern in design by turn-of-the-century standards, also housed a library for mill hands and students. In terms of length of school term and facilities, it was superior to Greer's own graded school.*

United Order of Odd Fellows in 1897, reserving a room for possible use as a school. In 1900, Pleasant Grove and Chick Springs were the only parts of District 9 that had schools for African-American children.

While schools and churches provided an improved quality of life for Greer, the community also had to provide for law enforcement. For its first 15 years or so, Greer did not require a regular officer because of its small size and tiny population. By around 1890, with 11 stores, outbuildings, churches, school, depot, and post office, the town saw the need to employ a night marshal. The first to hold this position was David Hoke Carman, a blacksmith and son of O'Neal Trial Justice John M. Carman. Recommended to the town council by merchant Cunningham Pennington in 1889, Carman also held a commission as a state constable. J.D. DeShields succeeded Carman around 1895 and continued in the post until the town's first police chief was hired.

New citizens brought business and enterprise, but also opinions that varied from tradition. The Templar influence had kept Greer relatively dry and quiet for many years. Most citizens opposed alcohol sales or consumption; some were active in the prohibition movement. At the state prohibition convention scheduled in Columbia

*CARMAN BLACKSMITH SHOP. John Landrum Carman was the first blacksmith in town, opening shop in 1874 on two original lots of the Shumate survey north of the railroad tracks on Trade Street. Carman was succeeded in the business by his brother David in 1905. The shop operated for 45 years.*

for June 7, 1894, Dr. B.F. Few of Greer, one of two vice presidents of the Greenville County chapter, attended. By the 1890s, however, diversity of opinion, at least on the subject of alcohol, appeared in Greer. Reputable citizens could take an open stand on behalf of liberalizing liquor laws. In fact, when the Dispensary Act was passed in 1897, a petition was presented in Greer to have the town declared the site of a state dispensary. The town split over the issue. The correspondent from Greer for the *Greenville Enterprise and Mountaineer* noted it would be a hard fight, suggesting a near-even match. Although a dispensary was never opened in Greer by this time, the town had clearly moved away from its earlier temperance stance.

During the early 1900s, Greer remained clearly united in opposition on the issues of barrooms and bootlegging. Personal and private drinking habits and legitimate trade in spirits were not generally opposed. Greer even had a small brewery, operated during the first decade of the century by W.M. Miller. Viewed from the outside by 1901, however, Greer was edging back toward its wild and rowdy past. It encouraged comparison with larger centers of hard-drinking and easy availability of illegal spirits like Charleston. Greer also attracted champions of morality. The Reverend J.R. Vaughn of Charlotte preached temperance on the town square in August 1901, the site of much of Greer's commerce in illicit spirits. The square was a regular site for street preachers for decades afterwards.

Most of the time, Greer's streets were generally quiet, most of its rowdiness attributed to complications arising from drunkenness or related in other ways to the whiskey and hard cider trade. The source of much of the whiskey was the Dark Corner. Foothill and mountain people who came to the mills brought their culture, conflicts, and connections along with them, including a strong penchant for use and consumption of alcohol, legal or not. Constables raided suspected blind tigers, or liquor houses, outside of Greer town limits, but were too few in numbers to control the trade. A raid at Arlington Cotton Mill village on Wednesday, July 2, 1902 prompted officers to go to Greer where they inspected the homes of Cole Dobson, Jim Brown, and Watt Nobles, finding empty containers at Dobson's house, but no alcohol. A letter appeared in the *Greenville Daily News* a few days later, signed "Citizens of Glassy Mt.," suggesting that whiskey was a recognized medium of exchange. "It is represented to be the means of paying Mr. Davenport, Greers, S. C., his fertilizer bill."

McDuff L. Littlefield, hired as Greer's first police chief in 1900, was assisted by night officer DeShields until late 1901. There was an interim of undetermined

*THE CARMAN FAMILY. Nora Belle P. Carman, wife of blacksmith David Hoke Carman, earned extra money for her family as a seamstress between 1890 and 1915. Children are, from left, Marie (with glasses), Alliene, Dollie (on mother's lap), and Frank.*

duration, ending on January 28, 1902 when the town was without a night officer. In spring 1903, the cider issue arose anew and the town council instructed Chief Littlefield to warn those violating town ordinances. Littlefield, a giant of a man, inspected wagons arriving in Greer and earned the respect of most visitors by his impartial enforcement of the law. By the turn of the century, however, Greer was bustling with people and business. Its cotton market attracted hundreds of farmers during the seasons of preparation and harvest. Drovers continued to arrive at Greer into the first decade of the new century, and the businesses generally thrived with some stores open from early morning until ten at night or later, six days a week. Simply keeping a watchful eye on things during the busiest daylight hours was beyond the ability of one man. Within two years of hiring its first full-time officer, Greer found it necessary to hire additional policemen.

Dependable law enforcement encouraged business development. Because of unrecorded data, lost records, and the amazing transience of dreamers who set up shop for the briefest periods in Greer, a complete accounting of all the business ventures is unattainable. Instead, what follows is an attempt to portray Greer's growth and development in terms of business trends, influence of visionary citizens, representative businesses, and the general progress of the town as revealed by the variety and novelty of enterprises.

When the Greer property was offered, many early shopkeepers kept their country stores or farms against the possibility that the new town might fail. John Carman bought lots in Greer in 1874, intending to move his blacksmith shop from O'Neal, but sent his oldest son instead. Simeon Hughes retained his farm at Bailey's Crossroads while he sold merchandise as the co-owner of a general store in Greer. H.C. Mark owned two businesses in Greenville when he invested in a Greer lot. William A. Hill of Enoree retained a farm against an uncertain mercantile business. He invested in real estate as well, as a hedge against mercantile failure. David D. Davenport, who co-owned a business before going it alone, also spread his investment money into real estate, cotton ginning, the cotton oil business, and later into insurance and Greenville real estate. Caution was the watchword and diversity of interest characterized Greer businessmen of the 1870s and early 1880s.

Persistence paid off for the earliest businesses in Greer. By 1880, J.L. Carman, who got his start in 1874, had built a house on the property and employed two African-American apprentices to help him. H.C. Mark retained his first lot, bought additional land in 1876, and opened H.C. Mark and Company, a mercantile business that continued to prosper two decades after the bars were closed. Simeon Hughes and W. Bomar bought lot 15 of the Shumate tract, set up the first general store on what is now the southeast corner of Trade and Victoria Streets (the present-day Bailey building), and sold out to William C. Bailey the next year. Hughes continued to invest in other businesses through the turn of the century.

Once Greer began to expand, another round of profits became possible from real estate. Shumate's lots were sold again and again, larger tracts undergoing subdivision, as business concentrated on Trade Street north of the depot. William

A. Hill, whose grandfather had come from Rhode Island with mill builder John Weaver, was the first major speculator in Greer real estate and the town's earliest major merchant. In 1874, Hill, who came from the Enoree community in Spartanburg County, bought lot 45, consisting of 36.5 acres or about one-fifth of the new town. Hill and John W. Cunningham formed a partnership in 1875 to open a general store, but later separated. Although Hill suffered serious business reversal, he made a rapid recovery and was doing business as a fertilizer dealer and general merchant in Greer by 1880. He also owned a cotton gin, a livery stable, and a drugstore, operated by Dr. D.C. Bennett. The Village Drug Store, which he later sold to Dr. B.F. Few, opened in 1882. Hill sold his corner store to H.P. Moore for $1,800. In 1884, Hill bought a farm from Legrand Zimmerman north of Greer for $3,135 and briefly engaged in cotton farming. In July of the following year, he had a good crop of cotton and had laborers clearing new ground for expanded cotton planting in 1886. He planned to petition the post

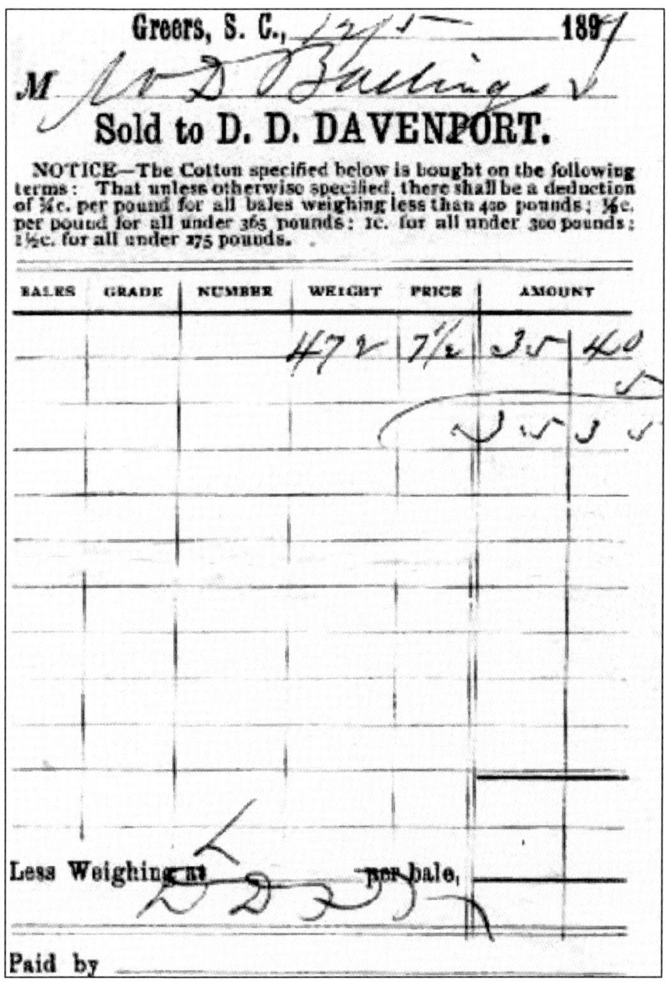
Greers, S. C., 189

M

Sold to D. D. DAVENPORT.

NOTICE—The Cotton specified below is bought on the following terms: That unless otherwise specified, there shall be a deduction of ¼c. per pound for all bales weighing less than 400 pounds; ½c. per pound for all under 365 pounds; 1c. for all under 300 pounds; 1½c. for all under 275 pounds.

| BALES | GRADE | NUMBER | WEIGHT | PRICE | AMOUNT |
|---|---|---|---|---|---|

Less Weighing at per bale,

Paid by

*D.D. DAVENPORT, COTTON BUYER. This cotton receipt is from D.D. Davenport, Greer's first millionaire and philanthropist, who made his fortune in diverse enterprises including cotton brokerage, cotton seed milling, and real estate.*

office department to establish a branch at his farm, Hilldale. Apparently faced with an offer he could not refuse, Hill instead sold the land to D.I. Collins only three months later for $5,000 and returned to his mercantile business in Greer where he sold fertilizer in partnership with Freno Dilling and Phillip Baker of Cleveland County, North Carolina. As a prosperous merchant, he built a large brick home on the southwest corner of Emma and Broad.

Cotton gins and sawmills were among the busiest places in Greer during the 1880s. W.E. Carver operated a steam-powered saw and planing mill and a cotton gin that ginned 190 bales. W.D. Smith, Simeon Hughes, and others invested in an engine cotton gin at a cost of $1,400 and set it in front of Smith's house. W.P. Taylor began operations in 1882 with an eight-horse steam engine that pulled a 36-inch blade. With three helpers, he cut up to 3,000 feet of lumber per day, selling oak on the Greenville market. The next year, he built a corn mill, since the closest one at the time was that of Spartan Mosteller. Taylor moved his operation closer to Greer by early 1884, locating between town and his competition, a sawmill run by Smith and Hughes. Both mills stayed busy during Greer's initial building boom. Jesse Cannon set up a sawmill in early 1885 and later equipped it to offer both rough and finished lumber to the growing town. Cannon had also been in the brick-making business since 1881 or earlier, making ceramic jugs as well as various jar ware.

When Greer was surveyed, Cunningham Pennington, a Confederate veteran (sergeant in Hampton's Legion), was a farmer and country storeowner in the O'Neal community. He bought the lot on the southwest corner of Trade and Victoria Streets for a new house, which was nearing completion in April 1882. Once the house was completed, Pennington, a dry goods and grocery merchant, rented spare rooms to mountain drovers and supplied pens and corrals behind his house for their flocks and herds. The shortage of housing prompted L.C. Zimmerman to open a boardinghouse near the depot.

During the 1880s, Greer attracted business for blacksmiths. Gabriel M. Davis bought a lot for his shop on Mosteller Street from Jesse Cannon by May 1885, and was doing business by early the next year. He joined John Landrum Carman, who was then beginning his second decade in Greer. In early 1887, T.M. Baswell moved his blacksmithing business from Cedar Hill to Greer.

David D. Davenport, another country merchant and Confederate veteran, was attracted to Greer and the opportunities it portended. Born in North Carolina, Davenport later operated a general store near Holly Springs before coming to Greer. He briefly served as postmaster at Mountain Ridge in Spartanburg County in 1875. Davenport moved to town, became a partner in a mercantile company, invested in land, and built one of the first large brick homes, completed by early 1881. Davenport's home served as a hotel catering to salesmen. He developed his lots on the south end of Greer by constructing stables and store buildings that he then rented. Wyatt and Company leased a large feed and livery stable for a number of years. After he bought out his partner, he was doing a $100,000 business in dry goods and groceries by 1890. In spring 1885, he built and operated a cotton gin.

He had been a cotton buyer in the Greer market from its beginning. By the end of the first decade of the twentieth century, he had expanded his investments to include Greenville realty. He became a partner in American Home Fire Insurance Company, being the only non-cotton mill man on the board, and served with Lewis Parker and other mill builders of Greer and Greenville. Davenport became Greer's first millionaire. In his later life, he contributed heavily to charity, founding a home for girls and providing much of the funding for a new high school, which was built after his death.

Hezekiah P. Moore, a veteran of the Union Army from Tennessee and an unapologetic Republican, came to Greer from Cleveland's Mill in late 1884. He rented William Hill's corner store and opened a general store some time after October 1, 1884. In 1887, he bought a half-acre lot from Hill, added to the existing building, and became Greer's first furniture dealer of record. He went into

*WILLIAM DRAYTON EDWARDS, BLACKSMITH. Edwards, one of Greer's last blacksmiths, is shown at the door of his shop, which was located near the middle of town.*

partnership with John F. Zimmerman, operating as H.P. Moore and Company, general mercantile in 1888. In 1892, he sold two-thirds interest in the property to Isaac L. Greene, who had retired from cotton manufacturing at Arlington.

J.D. Wood, who had been a highly successful tenant on the farm of Simeon Hughes at Bailey Crossroads, built a 3,000-square-foot livery stable in partnership with Hughes on Randal Street in late summer 1890. Although the business was called Hughes & Wood's, Hughes sold his interest to E.P. Wyatt by 1891. Wyatt's stable burned in December 1894. Wood married the daughter of D.D. Davenport, Clara May, who died young. Wood remarried, this time to his sister-in-law Pearl McLaughter. J.D. Wood and postmaster Isham Mayfield formed a partnership in a mercantile business and operated until January 7, 1907, when Mayfield sold out his interest to J. Terry Wood, who borrowed $2,550 from D.D. Davenport to buy Mayfield's interest. The old firm became known then as Wood & Wood. By 1909, the general merchandise store employed 13 people and did over $88,000 worth of business. In 1902, J.D. Wood began to offer undertaking services as his primary business after he bought out the funeral line of Greer Furniture and established Wood's Mortuary.

*TERRY WOOD. J. Terry Wood, a Reidville farmer, operated a general store in Greer. He later partnered with L.A. Stone and others in the Wood-Mendenhall Company.*

*PARTNERS. Greer Furniture Company began operations in 1901. L.A. Stone, J. Verne Smith, and W.D. McCorkle were original partners shown here in comic pose.*

William M. Ballenger, who began a mercantile business in 1890, did well with cash business with local citizens, as well as supplying many farmers during the summer. He rented a building and boarded with Mrs. Victoria Bailey, widow of W.C. Bailey. By 1893, Ballenger was actively buying and selling cotton, as well as general merchandise, both to mill agents and directly to cotton mills, such as Gaffney Manufacturing Company. In 1896, Ballenger bought Hill's store on the southwest corner lot of Broad and Emma (West Poinsett and South Main) from Nevassa Guano Company. He operated the store until his death in 1928. When his heirs closed the business, it was the oldest in Greer at the time.

One of the town's most enduring enterprises, Greer Cotton Seed Oil and Fertilizer Company, was chartered in 1896 by David D. Davenport. Oliver Palmer Smith managed the business, which began crushing cotton seeds in December of that same year, providing a new source of income for farmers. Reportedly, the first cottonseed oil extraction was done in South Carolina, and markets for the oil and byproducts developed during the last third of the nineteenth century. The cotton oil business was surprisingly profitable, considering that it had been common practice for farmers up to a few years after the Civil War to dump quantities of seed to rot or wash away in rivers. At Greer, the profits returned original investments to shareholders at the rate of 15 percent per annum at the turn of the century.

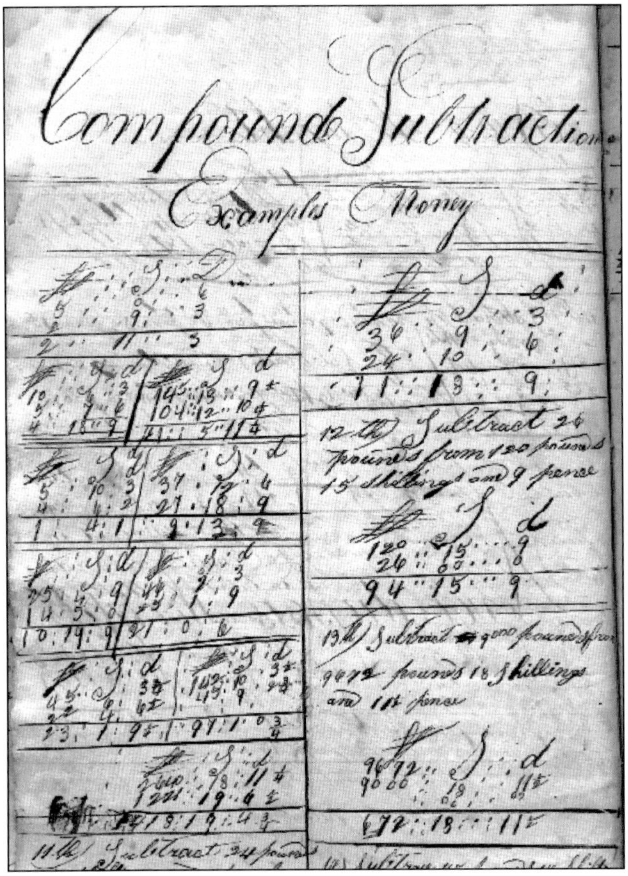


*WILLIAM BALLENGER'S COPY BOOK. William D. Ballenger, born in 1804, settled on a farm just east of the latter day Dogwood Acres community in 1838. The page shown is from his copybook, a loose-bound collection of practice exercises he accumulated as a school boy. William D. Ballenger, who had no significant connection with William M. Ballenger—apart from the similarity of their names—was a farmer whose descendants worked the same lands north of Greer for 125 years.*

Four marketable products were derived from the business when ginning was included: oil, linters, meal, and hulls. The oil was sold at prices ranging from 24¢ to 37¢ per gallon to Atlantic Oil, American Cotton Oil Company, and Southern Cotton Oil Company, and shipped by rail to Savannah, Atlanta, and other points along the Southern and its connectors. Crushed cottonseed was sold as meal for feed and fertilizer applications to farmers at $1.10 per sack and the hulls sold at 3¢ per pound. Linters were sold for batting at the rate of 4¢ to 4.25¢ per pound. Meal and oil were the primary products from the processing of cottonseed. From a ton of seed, it is calculated that 38 gallons of oil, 1,177 pounds of hulls, and 785 pounds of meal could be salvaged. In October 1901, buyers bought seed at 70¢ per hundred pounds. The cotton oil business was seasonal, beginning in earnest in October and lasting usually through March. In addition to the oil press, Greer Fertilizer Company later bought the fertilizer operation.

After fire destroyed the Oil Mill office and warehouse buildings, a new stone and mortar office building was constructed on the east side of the property. After Davenport's death, the heirs and sitting directors sold the stock to a new corporation, Greer Oil Mill and Feed Company, Inc. Capitalized at $100,000 on

September 21, 1922, it continued ginning operations until 1959. During the early 1960s, a livestock auction operated on the premises and continued to operate in some form well into the 1980s.

Just two years after the Oil Mill was built, E.S. Brooks of Pennsylvania, along with local investors L.J. Green, HP. Moore, W.E. Waldrop, and J.A. Robinson, chartered the Brooks Manufacturing Company on May 9, 1898. Brooks supplied the working capital and know-how; Green supplied the property. The batting mill located on Line Street just north of the Southern Railroad tracks did business for five years before it failed. It reopened under new management, but again closed after two years.

Another long-term town business is the Greer Lumber Company, which opened for business in 1897 under the name of L.J. Green & Sons. Around mid-July, construction began on their office on Hill Street (East Poinsett) at the approximate site of the Dixie Shoe Shop, once occupied by John McMurray's Western Auto Associate Store. The yards were to the rear of the store. After opening, L.J. Green remained active in the business until shortly before his death in 1913. A. Mahaffey and T.H. Brockman, Green's son-in-law, bought the business (by then called Greer Lumber Company) from Green around July 1910. The company bought lumber and moldings from Waldeman & Sons among other sawmills then dotting the midlands of the state. In 1929, J.F. Fleming and W.C. Smith chartered a second firm named Greer Lumber Company. For decades, it was located on the west side of South Main Street beside the Piedmont & Northern (P&N) tracks.

*GREER OIL MILL SEED WAREHOUSE. Greer Cotton Seed Oil & Fertilizer Company was chartered in 1896. The cotton oil business was surprisingly profitable, returning original investments to shareholders at the rate of 15% per annum at the turn of the century.*

The businessman who best preserved the history of Greer in pictures was Charlie W. Drace, who arrived in Greer from Gettysburg, Pennsylvania in 1896 to form a partnership with A.P. Farmer and establish Greer's first photography studio. Drace bought Farmer's interest in January 1902. Drace had reason to settle as he had met Fannie Miller, a local girl, courted her, and married her on Tuesday, January 5, 1897. He exhibited some of the first moving pictures and opened the Grand, the first theater in Greer, which he operated until his sons entered the business. Drace, who was a first-class portrait photographer, billed himself in advertisements as an artist. He also did scenic photography for the developing postal card business, photographing views in North Carolina for the American View Company of Charlotte. He later did a series of local scenes that he self-published.

Communication arrived in Greer when telephone lines extended from Greer to Batesville and Pelham in 1889, and to Chick Springs in 1890. Local phone service, however, consisted only of a drop from existing lines to a very few subscribers. A telephone line connecting Greenville and Spartanburg via Hammett Bridge Road was begun on April 17, 1893. The Greer telephone exchange began operating in 1899. Annie Pennington, daughter of Cunningham Pennington, was the first operator and ran a switchboard from her mother's house located on Victoria Street. There were only 25 drops on the first board, including lines to Victor Mill Company Store, J.D. Wood, D.D. Davenport, the Bank of Greers, Andreas' Store at O'Neal, H.B. Ingram, W.W. Burgess, T.E. Smith, W.M. Ballenger, and Gilreath's farm. In 1909, David Davenport leased a building for an exchange on Main Street to the telephone company. Annie Pennington, the sole operator for ten years, operated the exchange from seven in the morning until ten at night six days a week. Sunday calls could be made if necessary, but were generally frowned upon as calling times were carefully circumscribed by the hours of church service, Miss Pennington being a devout Baptist.

By the late 1880s, Greer had attracted four doctors. Dr. Henry V. Westmoreland, Greer's first physician, began a country practice about 1870. Dr. Ben F. Few followed Dr. Westmoreland; Drs. T.R. League and E.M. Rose arrived by 1888. Greer's correspondent wrote the *Greenville Enterprise and Mountaineer* on December 24, 1890, "all we need is a bank and a court house, for we have plenty of preachers of all denominations and doctors thrown in." Dr. W.E. Walker arrived in 1889. By mid-1895, Dr. James R. Durham had a practice and Dr. T.E. Cunningham, Dr. Westmoreland's son-in-law, arrived in 1897. Dr. Madison A. Drummond, Greer's first dentist, began practicing in 1898. Drummond, a native of Woodruff, was a University of Tennessee graduate.

In 1900, another University of Tennessee Medical School graduate, Dr. Fred G. James, came to practice medicine in Greer. Licensed to practice in 1894, James first served the Milford community. When he moved to Greer in 1903, he had a home built on West Poinsett Street from which he ran his practice. In 1906, he became a partner in the Highland Drug Company and continued his practice for another four decades.

*DR. CUNNINGHAM. Dr. Theron Earle Cunningham, early Greer physician, is shown in his buggy about to make rounds in Greer. Dr. Cunningham died in 1900.*

When Greer was incorporated in 1876, its agricultural economy was largely based upon the promise and exchange of cotton. Most citizens had little need for banks as they rarely saw cash even when it came time to settle accounts at the fall harvest. Only around the turn of the century did the new mills and diversity of business create a need for banking services. Before the establishment of regular banking houses, it was common practice for mercantile companies to provide limited forms of banking services for their clientele. Farmers gave liens on their crops to merchants in exchange for advances of seed, fertilizers, ploughs, necessary household goods, and occasionally cash. At harvest, they were credited with crops, primarily cotton, which was increasingly grown as a cash crop in the upstate after the Civil War.

For a quarter of a century after its founding, Greer remained dependent upon Greenville and Spartanburg for its banking needs beyond the simple services general store merchants could offer. Some interest in a local bank began to develop by the late 1880s after Greer, although still small by any standard, had become established as both a fertilizer terminal, supplying farmers particularly in the northern county, and a cotton market in its own right.

In April 1890, the *Greenville Enterprise and Mountaineer* reported that W.C. Moore and Greer postmaster A.J. Creighton had completed incorporation papers for the Farmers Bank that would be located at Greers. The capital stock was $25,000, to be issued in shares at $50 each. This information could not be confirmed through the office of the Secretary of State, and this bank disappears from public record after this newspaper report. In September of that year, Dr. Creighton resigned from the post office because of poor health, which may have been a factor in a decision not to follow through with the bank. He died the next year.

By the end of the century, Lewis W. Parker became the force behind the first bank organized in Greer. The town's leading cotton buyers joined Parker and his law partner Harry Haynesworth in the organization of a bank. They submitted a petition to the Secretary of State in December 1899 and chartered in February of the next year. Dr. Benjamin F. Few, William H. Ballenger, Thomas E. Smith, Harry J. Haynesworth, Chaney Littlefield, W.W. Burgess, and Lewis Parker served as the original board of directors. The Bank of Greers, which was the first Greenville County bank outside of the city of Greenville, was capitalized at $30,000 and served a small public. Business grew slowly but steadily with capitalization rising to $50,000 in less than ten years. The bank was located originally on Trade Street, one lot down from the southwest corner of Trade and Victoria, until early 1905 when a new building was completed on the northwest corner of the intersection. By the end of 1906, the bank had accumulated a surplus greater than its original capital stock and had paid an 8 percent dividend to investors.

The need for banking institutions grew with the development of modern cotton mills in Greer. In the spring of 1894, Wesley W. Burgess, John Robinson, and Dr. Henry V. Westmoreland initiated a movement to build a cotton mill just outside Greer town limits. A significant part of the argument for a local mill was the availability of cotton within wagon-hauling distance. H.D. Wheat, founder of Gaffney Manufacturing Company, served as a consultant and met with the

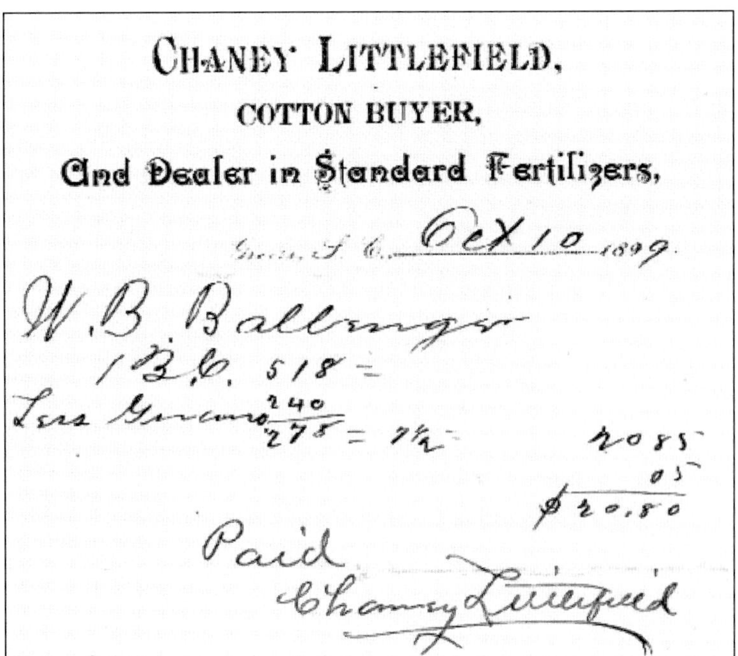
CHANEY LITTLEFIELD,
COTTON BUYER,
And Dealer in Standard Fertilizers,
Greers, S. C. Oct 10 1899
W. B. Ballenger
1 B.C. 518 =
= 7½ 20 85
05
$20.80
Paid
Chaney Littlefield

*CHANEY LITTLEFIELD, COTTON BUYER. Littlefield, a cotton buyer and fertilizer dealer, was instrumental in building Greer's first commercial cotton warehouse.*

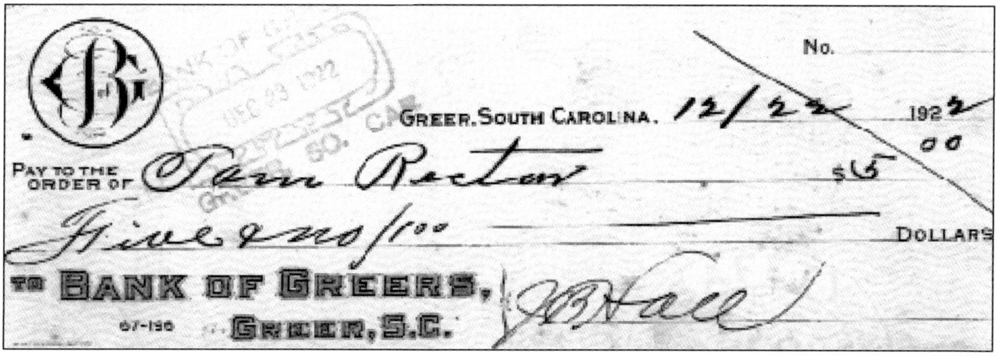


*BANK OF GREERS. The Bank of Greers was organized in 1899 to meet the banking demands of a cotton mill and growing cotton market, which often gave better prices for the staple than did either Greeville or Spartanburg buyers.*

promoters the first week of May. He promised to raise $100,000 if local investors could promise $50,000. He recommended producing a finer grade of goods than those generally made in southern cotton mills. To produce such a product, the mill would have to have the latest machinery and would likely require bringing in experienced northern mill workers.

Greer investors decided to move forward with the project despite the risks; however, they were having trouble raising the money. By February, they had raised only $35,000, but information about the project began to trickle into public conversation. Local gossip suggested that a prominent mill man from Greenville would be offered the top position. If capital was in doubt, there was no doubt about the location or the abundant supply of raw material. By 1895, Greer had a prosperous cotton market, and many bales that once went to Greenville were going to Greer instead for a better price. The typical 6,000-plus bales handled at Greer in an average season was more than equal to the needs of most existing mills.

By summer, the initial money was subscribed and the project was ready to begin. Edward Moseley, veteran African-American brickmaker, arrived in early August to begin making an estimated 2 million bricks needed for the first phase of construction, scheduled to be completed by January 1896. M.L. Marchant, Noah Cannon, J.H. Payne, David Cannon, Thaddeus T. Westmoreland, W.M. Ballenger, W.E. Waldrop, S. Hughes, Henry V. Westmoreland, L. Jackson Green, W.E. Burgess, and E.P. Wyatt chartered the Victor Manufacturing Company in the summer of 1895. Burgess was elected president and secretary; J.W. Kendrick was named vice president. Installation of machinery continued into the spring of 1897, and some cloth was being produced by April. All looms were operational by the second week of May.

Of the principals, Martin Luther Marchant was the most knowledgeable and experienced in cotton mill operations. Marchant had arrived in Greenville County from Graniteville, the state's premier cotton factory, to work at Batesville, one of the oldest operations in the state. He had remained there until it passed from the original owner's control. Marchant, the only member of the investors with extensive cotton mill experience, died in January 1897 before the mill was fully operational. The other investors included a farmer, grocer, physician, general merchant, and cotton broker. Education levels of the group ranged from illiterate to post graduate; yet, they held in common the funds and the desire to invest in the cotton mill business.

Two years passed from the planning stage to the operational stage, a little longer than some of the original investors had anticipated. An indication of marketing difficulty may be inferred from the fact that the company offered a large stock of goods to the local market through merchant H.P. Moore. Goods were also sold at the company store; nevertheless, by late summer, the company was $60,000 in debt.

After Burgess resigned as president, Lewis W. Parker took the position. A former schoolteacher, Parker became an attorney and entered practice in Greenville in 1888. He and his partner Harry J. Haynesworth represented Greenville cotton manufacturers and developed an enthusiasm for the business. Because of his expertise in cotton mill financial operation, he was offered the position and brought stability and innovation to the company. After refinancing the debt with the issuance of $100,000 of preferred stock, he had an additional 5,000 spindles installed for increased production.

The largest textile operation in Greer from its beginning, Victor was a dynamic place to live and work during the first 50 years of its existence. In 1898, the plant consisted of a vertically organized three-story mill. Carding was done on the second floor, spinning on the third, and weaving on the first. At the northeast corner were warehouses, and a cloth room was attached at the southwest corner of the mill. Its complement of machinery included 940 looms, 1,050 spindles, 2 spoolers, 3 nappers, a slasher, 16 cards, 36 drawing-in frames, 2 stubbers, 12 speeders, 3 pickers, and 4 intermediates. Although the engine room was originally designed for the first floor, a separate steam engine room was built in less than five years. The power train of the mill consisted of a steam engine and the master drive wheel, which weighed 65,000 pounds. From that axle, belts ran to machinery on each floor.

With the expansion of the mill in several phases came the building of accommodations for the workers. In the fall of 1901, homes for the overseers were built. Superintendent H.F. Moody, originally from Brunswick, Maine, moved into a new, larger home. The building of the Victor Manufacturing Company and its village set Greer on the road to an industrial town at the turn of the century.

# 4. Progressive Greer: 1900–1917

Historians consider the period 1890 to 1917 the Progressive Era of United States history because of the prevailing notion of the time that virtually all civic problems could be addressed with reason, education, and appropriate legislation. Reformers worked to improve conditions in education, promote women's suffrage, eliminate child labor, develop more responsive local governments, and defeat the vices. During these years, Greer was experiencing both the progressive spirit and a local economic boom. As Greer changed, the need for regulation and public services became evident. The public wanted cultural and social activities as well, while it struggled with social and racial issues. During the same period, Greer expanded its business center by attracting a second railway line, building banks, and opening more textile mills.

Greer citizens knew no limits to the progress that the small but booming New South town was capable of reaching. In 1904, citizens decided to change the system of municipal government from the outdated intendant/warden form to the mayor/alderman plan. The change of government required the election of six aldermen, but only four were elected in 1905. A special election was called to elect the additional two. In the mayoral race, J.F. Gilreath defeated longtime trial justice Thaddeus T. Westmoreland by a margin of 95 to 1.

By the end of that year, the issue of women's suffrage was being addressed. To vote in elections, a person had to be male and over 20 years of age. Residency requirements were two years in the state, one year in the county, and four months in Greer. On Christmas Day, 1905, a demonstration on behalf of suffrage was held in Greer.

During the twentieth century, the town council began the practice of electing the chief of police and other city employees annually after city elections. Chief Littlefield was an effective officer and was reelected as long as he wanted the job. He was paid a salary of $40 a month out of which he bought his own uniform. Although the chief had an assistant for the daylight shift, the job of night patrolman was difficult to keep filled. In 1904, Littlefield hired William Foster, a farmer, for the night shift. J.D. DeShields, former town marshal, continued to work for Littlefield as a day officer for two more years. These officers were limited in their jurisdiction to the town limits, a problem for Greer since bootleggers often brought whiskey wagons to the edge of town to sell their wares. Too few constables and county officers left enforcement to the local police, who nabbed miscreants when they ventured into town.

The small force became known for its no-nonsense enforcement of liquor laws. Littlefield's personal reputation, enhanced by his size and ability to handle the roughest characters, became a challenge to men who had in some cases brought their spirits to Greer for years. The years 1904 to 1906 were critical for law enforcement in Greer as the chief and his tiny force determined that law and order would prevail.

On Saturday night, July 2, 1904, Chief Littlefield assigned Night Officer William Foster to keep watch for a whiskey wagon rumored to be headed to Greer from the Dark Corner. Foster, a married man with two young children, was required to furnish his own uniform. On this night for the first time, he was wearing the

*PATROLMAN FOSTER. Greer officer William Foster poses for a portrait taken in brand new uniform the day he was killed in the line of duty.*

suit, which he had picked up at a tailor's shop earlier in the day. Before reporting to work, Foster had stopped by Drace's Studio and had himself photographed in his new uniform, the portrait to be a present for his wife Mattie.

Saturday was a big day for farmers and merchants; the town was filled early and many remained late. Since most of the stores were open, the town was still lively hours after sunset. About 10 p.m., Foster was observed standing near Sturdivant's Store in mid-block of Hill Street just south of the intersection of Emma and Mosteller Streets. He crossed the street walking toward Basewell's blacksmith shop and a grove of trees beyond. Shortly thereafter, a number of people still on the street heard reports of three shots fired in rapid succession. Bill Pennington, local painting contractor, was at Sturdivant's when the shots were fired. Running toward the sound, he was first on the scene about 100 yards north of Sturdivant's and found Foster lying face-down and unconscious with his feet in the street. Pennington noticed that Foster had not drawn his pistol.

When the shooting happened, mill man William W. Burgess went to the scene, which was poorly lit from Sturdivant's Store lights. He sent for a lantern. Near Foster's prone form, Burgess noticed two whiskey bottles: a Clark & Sons commercial bottle and a South Carolina Dispensary Flask. T.C. Wakefield, who operated a men's clothing store, later testified that he had heard a voice cry out after the shooting, "Pour it to him."

Dr. Henry Westmoreland was summoned. When he arrived, he pronounced Foster dead at the scene. The body was carried to Dr. Fred James's home and office on Emma Street where Doctors Westmoreland and James performed a midnight autopsy on the fallen officer. Foster had been hit twice by the gunfire. The fatal bullet entered between the second and third ribs, punctured the heart, and exited between the sixth and seventh ribs. A second bullet fractured the left elbow.

The man suspected of shooting Foster was Boyce Stone, a young man in his early 20s who was supposed to have been driving the rumored whiskey wagon. While Stone had some grudge against Littlefield, it was not known that he had enmity for Foster. He owned and frequently carried a .41-caliber Colt pistol. In his late teens, he had spent some time working in the wheat fields of Texas and Oklahoma. When he returned to South Carolina, he found work hauling and selling bootleg whiskey made in the upper county.

After Chief Littlefield conferred with Greenville County Sheriff Jefferson D. Gilreath, they agreed to pick up Stone. Littlefield and others believed that Stone had mistaken Foster for the chief in the dim light of the evening since Foster had not, until that night, worn a uniform on the job. Both Foster and Littlefield were large men. In the course of investigation, two of Stone's associates, T. Watt Nobles and George Downs, an African American, were also arrested for murder. Nobles and Downs were known bootleggers. Evidence against the suspects established that Nobles had been in Greer much of the day and had been seen leaving after the shooting. Nobles had also been heard making a threat against another town official, Mayor Gilreath. George Downs was observed running from the direction of the shots immediately after they were fired. Although the evidence was largely circumstantial, it sufficed to convince many local folk before the case came to trial.

The gunning down of Officer Foster created a public outcry for law and order. Six days after the shooting, a crowd of some 50 men rode up to the home of J.B. Fuller, brother-in-law of Watt Nobles. Members of the mob, composed of the town's leading citizens, surrounded and entered the home. Businessmen, cotton buyers, merchants, and others had formed a law and order league, visited those that the league deemed "undesirable," and ordered them out of town.

The days between the killing of Foster and the trial of his accused killers were particularly unsettled. Greer struggled to maintain order as it became difficult to keep police officers. After Foster was killed, Officer J.D. DeShields resigned. Two officers, Gus Mason and Ben Center, were hired as night police. Officer Center apparently left by October and was replaced by an Officer Morris. Morris and Mason apparently had misgivings about their responsibilities, but agreed to work through the current council's term that ended in February.

On September 18, 1904, a disturbance near Victor Mill village led to a confrontation between Greer authorities and a disorderly group of men from the Dark Corner area. Whether this incident was directly related to the Foster case is not clear. Mayor James Gilreath, backed by two Greer officers, ordered the men to raise their hands. In the confusion that followed, one of the men appeared to draw a gun and Gilreath opened fire with a double-barreled shotgun, wounding G.W. Alexander in the arm and face. He survived. Subsequently, Gilreath was charged with assault and battery with intent to kill. The case was first presented in Spartanburg County, but there was a question of jurisdiction since the incident took place near the county line. After Spartanburg relinquished the case to a Greenville County court, it was given a preliminary hearing scheduled for November 18, 1904. Gilreath was exonerated; no record of further prosecution appears.

As the date of his trial approached, Boyce Stone was described as confident of its outcome. Stone and his co-defendants went to trial on February 2, 1905. Nobles, expecting a strong case by the prosecution, mounted a spirited defense. There was confusion over the kind of gun Stone had in his possession on the night of Foster's murder and the caliber of the fatal bullet. Stone was known to have owned a specific make and caliber pistol, but that weapon was not found in his possession when he was arrested. It was argued that he could have exchanged guns with Nobles or with someone else. Other than circumstance and conjecture, evidence was sparse. The defense challenged the credibility of the prosecution's witnesses. A map of Greer, drawn by Augustus R. Wood, proprietor of Greer Oil Mill, showed the relative positions of witnesses when the shots were fired. None were close enough to see the shooting. The jury was out only one hour, returning with a verdict of not guilty. Fearful that friends of Officer Foster might try to avenge his death, Stone left the state.

Despite the determination of local citizens to support their law officers—even joining them to maintain order and deal with offenders—Greer remained particularly vulnerable to whiskey-related crime. Bootlegging continued as

*EARLY OFFICERS. Ben Center and Fowler Green (far right) were early police officers in Greer. The photo dates from about 1904.*

the bane of Greer, occasionally developing into or giving rise to more serious offenses. In 1999, Lewis Brewton, an African American, was drunk and armed. He began firing his pistol in the street, endangering the black community where he had parked his wagon. After Chief Littlefield was summoned, he walked toward Brewton empty handed. Brewton opened fire, getting off three shots before Littlefield got to his gun. Although the bullets ripped the chief's uniform, they did not injure him. Littlefield shot and mortally wounded Brewton, who continued firing while on the ground until his gun was empty. Littlefield was acquitted in General Sessions Court on January 23, 1906.

Boyce Stone left little doubt in the minds of most that it was he who had shot Foster. After his return from the West, he continued to traffic in whiskey, supplying both black and white communities, but generally remaining away from Greer. In summer 1908, Stone and two of his friends appeared at the home of an African American named Henry Fowler, who lived near Victor Mill. Fowler was inside the house when Stone, who had been drinking, walked into the yard to confront Fowler's wife. She urged Stone to leave, but he then advanced toward the woman, frightening her. When she ran into the house to alert her husband, Fowler came running from the house with a shotgun and fired, the balls breaking two of Stone's ribs and penetrating his lungs. Mortally wounded, Stone ran some 50 feet before he collapsed and died on the spot. Henry Fowler walked to Greer and turned himself in.

Dr. Fred James examined the body and gave the testimony that convicted Fowler. Both Fowler and his wife were arrested and charged with murder. The arrest of the Fowlers was good form, both in keeping with the custom of the times and possibly protecting them from violence by Stone's friends. The Fowler's bail bonds were raised almost immediately by leading businessmen of Greer. At his trial, Henry Fowler testified that he saw Stone in silhouette, thought he was drawing a gun, and shot in self-defense. Convicted of manslaughter on detailed evidence given by Dr. James, Fowler was given a minimum sentence. Stone, upon seeing the shotgun, had made his turn to run when the blast struck him in the side and back.

Patrolman Foster died in the line of duty at a time when officers had no employee benefits. Greer Town Council, however, provided for the funeral expense, placed a monument to the officer in Edgewood Cemetery, and helped Mattie Foster publicly and privately throughout the rest of her life, providing subsistence funds and money to meet doctor bills as needed. On August 1, 1905, the town council voted to begin paying for the uniforms of police officers.

*OFFICER'S WIDOW. Mattie P. Foster, left with two small children when her husband was gunned down in July 1904, found work as a store clerk to support her family.*

Several Greer ordinances were revised in 1905. The liquor law was broadened to include prohibition of the sale, possession, or transportation of contraband liquor. Gambling and prostitution were clearly prohibited and blue laws clarified.

Littlefield was again elected chief by the town council in 1905, and J.T. Paris and E.A. Bearden were named night officers. Bearden worked for a short time and resigned, again leaving the town short of lawmen. To guarantee order and demonstrate the town's support of its lawmen, the council passed an ordinance in March requiring citizens to assist with arrests when called on by an officer.

When David Ballenger was robbed and beaten on Sunday morning, June 27, 1905, a number of citizens tracked the assailant to Pelham. Magistrate James and Constable Taylor were with the posse when it captured an African American named Sam Hudson. The officials became separated from the group, some of whom began to cry out for a lynching. Hudson was tied to a tree and whipped, then turned over to officers. When they carried him to Greer, the crowd was still angry and growing. At Greer, with the danger of lynching growing by the hour, Hudson was taken to Greenville for lodging in a safer jail. Officers drove the prisoner in a carriage over the back roads to avoid being overtaken by the would-be lynch mob.

Chief Littlefield left the police force briefly to deal in real estate. L.A. Green, who served part of 1909 and 1910, succeeded him. Littlefield returned to the job in 1910. Despite the best efforts of an undermanned police department, whiskey problems continued to plague Greer. The town's location on the county line, its rapid growth, and the influx of population from the foothills and mountains made it difficult to enforce the laws effectively. Rising population brought in by the construction of four cotton mills between 1896 and 1910 brought not only more crime, but more serious crime. In 1917, Charlie Littlefield succeeded his brother McDuff as chief of police. The former chief returned to business and, some years later, was elected to city council.

The old Greer jailhouse, which had been used mainly to lock up those who indulged too much in moonshine, was torn down. The old lockup, known as the guardhouse, had two cells and was in bad shape, having been the victim of vandalism. Because it was so poorly heated, inmates were allowed out on the honor system to spend the nights at home and return the next morning. A new city hall complete with cellblock and offices was contracted to J.C. Cunningham in March 1917.

As the main downtown area became more defined with new construction, the likelihood of fire became greater. The town council passed an ordinance in January 1909 to define a fire line for wood construction, covering the south end of town. Bucket brigades had to rely on wells, horse troughs, and hand pumps to supply water that was never in sufficient volume to do more than wet down nearby buildings to keep fire from spreading. The Southern Hotel, operated by R.R. Jacobs near the depot, burned on September 17, 1907. A two-story house in operation as a hotel only a few months, it had no fire escapes. Second-floor guests managed to escape the flames on ladders set up for them.

The most threatening fire in Greer's brief history occurred on February 8, 1912, when a gas stove exploded in Yates' Restaurant, a small, wood-constructed place operated by E.C. Yates on Main Street. Flames spread rapidly to Charles Dobbins's livery stable at the rear of the restaurant. The livestock were saved, but the fire continued to spread to the warehouse and stables of Greer Furniture Store. Volunteers fought the fire all day by bucket brigade. Greenville was alerted that Greer's main trading center might be destroyed. With neither water mains nor hydrants to supply a stream, Greenville equipment was of little help.

As many as 200 men and boys manned buckets supplied from wells as the flames threatened the entire town. The livery stable contained over 7,500 square feet and was entirely in flames at the height of the danger. Observers agreed that T.W. Glenn was a hero as he stood at the fire's edge, dowsing water into the flames. His clothes caught fire several times. After several hours, a change in the wind direction prevented more of the town from being consumed. After about 18 hours of hand-to-hand efforts by virtually every male in Greer large enough to lug a bucket, the fire was finally brought under control. Less than a month after the fire, the council enacted an ordinance prohibiting construction other than masonry, brick, or stone along the business streets, including Hill, Trade, and Emma. The next year, fires again plagued Greer, but not in such a spectacular manner. Although the fires were small, they were numerous, with fire losses for April 1913 more than those of Greenville.

After another major fire, which threatened to sweep through Franklin Mill village, the Greer Fire Department was organized in 1914. The village, closest mill community to the new large and beautiful homes on Emma Street, lost three houses completely. Fire severely damaged another house before Greer citizens and villagers brought the fire under control. No lives were lost due to the quick thinking of neighbors, who carried a disabled man from one of the houses. After the Greer Council asked Chief R.J. Legon of the Greenville Fire Department to advise them in setting up a department, he spent several days in Greer in August 1914, assisting officials in selecting firefighting equipment. The fire department was funded by the town, but manned by an all-volunteer force into the 1920s, a chief being elected annually by firefighters. Ordinarily, volunteers numbered around 25. William Pennington, a painting contractor, was elected as first chief. G.W. Hoesch, a meat cutter at Julius Hughes's Union Meat Market, succeeded him.

The earliest equipment for fighting fires in Greer consisted of "pumpers," carts with mounted pumps and tanks, which were designed to be horse drawn, but could be quickly attached to an automobile as well. In the event of a fire, any available car could be used for which the city paid the owner $1. The limits on this system were, first and foremost, availability of water near the scene of a fire since the capacity of the pumper was small. Other limiting factors included the volume of water, pressure, and access to the flames. Time of replenishing water figured into how much damage resulted from a fire.

Greer's pumper was initially housed on Hill Street before a municipal building was constructed on Randal Street on the north side of the Town Square in 1917.

The fire department was housed in the new city hall along with the city clerk's office and police and fire department offices on the ground floor. A courtroom and fire department supply and sleeping rooms were on the second floor, as well as an office for the public health officer. The first fire truck used in Greer, a Seagraves model, was obtained two years later. Despite legitimate fears based on real fire hazards in transition from oil lamp to electric light and from wood construction to masonry, the major fires like the one of 1912 were infrequent. A volunteer force was long sufficient for Greer's firefighting needs. With such infrequent use, it became the custom for a number of years to sound the fire whistle each morning at six.

Besides concern for public safety, public health concerns grew in Greer. In 1886, concern over a possible epidemic of diphtheria aroused public interest. A board of health in Greer was established as early as 1889 and continued to operate thereafter with members of Greer's medical practice and other citizens serving on the board. Members in 1897 included Dr. Henry Westmoreland, B.F. Few, and W.E. Walker. The board elected in February included J.A. Robinson, Lee Marchant, and T.M. Hill. In July, the council passed an ordinance requiring hogs and pigpens to conform to certain standards, to be kept clean and disinfected.

Greer's focus on prevention helped to avoid epidemics, for the most part, until the influenza outbreak of 1918. Spring and summer fevers were not uncommon in an age before antibiotics, and diphtheria robbed the crib quite

*PROGRESSIVE GREER. By the beginning of the First World War, Greer was prosperous and attractive. Almost all the lots on Trade Street had been taken by one form of business enterprise or another, as shown in this scene.*

often. Nor were physicians immune to the diseases they treated; Dr. and Mrs. Henry Westmoreland buried six of their seven children, all of whom died from diphtheria their father brought into the home on his clothes or hands. Smallpox, which occurred in the Greer area in 1898, was a general outbreak but of a relatively mild strain. Because many of the townspeople were vaccinated, the cases in Greer were few. In the countryside, especially near Pelham, hundreds of cases were reported.

Sanitation was the primary concern of the board of health during the years before public sewerage and water became available. Most residents kept a milk cow; some kept pigs and chickens for fresh meat and eggs; and most obtained water from public and private wells. Summer fevers, such as typhoid and scarlet, were fairly common before ordinances and plumbing reduced the risks. Citizens were assessed a fee of 25¢ per month for cleaning out and hauling away the contents of privies. In July 1906, citizens with hogs were required to keep them in pens with plank floors. Also addressed were problems such as stagnant water and rubbish. The keeping of hogs in the town limits was outlawed in August 1906, but not without some dissent. After the installation of public utilities and at the behest of a consensus at a mass meeting, the council passed an ordinance in 1916 requiring citizens to hook up to sewers or install a sanitary device within 30 days.

Besides human health, citizens were also concerned about animals' health and rights. Other than the Masons, one of the earliest civic groups in Greer, a branch of the Society for the Prevention of Cruelty to Animals (SPCA), organized on September 30, 1908, partly in response to a controversial court case arising from the charging of a Greer farmer with a series of violations the previous year. Fred Clark, a cotton farmer who lived on Mosteller Road, witnessed a young man beating his own horse as Clark drove his wagon home in April 1907. He stopped his wagon, approached the man, took the stick from his hand, led the horse a few yards away, and turned it loose. All of this happened under protests by the intimidated horse owner. The next day, Clark was charged with horse stealing. In magistrate's court on April 15, it was shown that the horse was not taken from its owner but merely turned loose and that the owner was able to catch it shortly thereafter. The case was dismissed. Unsatisfied, the owner had Clark arrested under a warrant for trespass. Again, the facts of the case were presented as before. On this occasion, a jury found Clark not guilty. Clark had borrowed money against his crop as was common among small farmers at the time. When it was determined that Clark had sold a bale of cotton and had not settled with his mortgagee, the horse owner informed the lein holder, who had Clark charged with disposing of a crop under lein. Trial was set for May 24. Again, Clark was ready to present his evidence, which was that the cotton bale sold and the crop under lein represented two different years. The prosecution did not appear for the case then, nor is there record of any continuance. Clark became something of a local hero for a time. Ironically, Clark, basically a shy man, did not join the SPCA that was composed largely of townsmen. Two years later, the town council passed an ordinance forbidding cruelty to animals within its corporate limits.

After saloons were outlawed, early visitors to Greer had little in the way of diversions other than church services. For 25 years, custom was sufficient to preserve Sunday as a day of worship and rest; yet, closing of barrooms alone was no guarantee of public stability. The conflict of generation and religious differences was manifested in an incident that occurred in the spring of 1886. A crowd of young men and women visited Gibbes Mill Pond at Gibbes Shoals near Batesville for a picnic with some fishing thrown in for good measure. Apparently, the fish weren't biting and the dancing began. The *Baptist Courier* got wind of the occurrence and editorially suggested that the Methodists in the crowd were leaders who encouraged dancing among Baptist girls.

Season permitting, the picnic was a common form of recreation. Bailey's Mineral Springs, located on the Simeon Hughes property, and Gibbs Shoals on Rocky Creek near Pelham, were sites easily within buggy travel distance for sweethearts, families in reunion, and classes about to dismiss for the term. Chick Springs resort dated to antebellum days and was a favorite recreational site for Greer folk. An easy buggy ride away, the resort on summer Sundays often had 150 buggies, wagons, and carriages parked under the oaks that shaded the springs below the hotel. After the P&N Railroad cut was made, it was a flat, smooth walk.

Jockey Day was the day set aside by custom, the first Saturday of the month when farmers and traders came to town to offer their products and swap livestock at the town square. The custom began in Greer in 1894 and all kinds of items, such as produce, guns, knives, dogs, and livestock, were sold or swapped. After the turn of the century, Greer's Jockey Day was changed to the first Monday of

*CHICK'S SPRINGS, EARLY SCENE. Chick's Springs resort, dating to antebellum days, was a favorite recreational site of Greer folk. An easy buggy ride away, it accomodated crowds of 300–500 who came to swim in the lake, picnic, or drink its legendary healthful waters bubbling up from several natural springs.*

*WOOD FAMILY REUNION 1914. The Wood family settled in the vicinity south of Bailey Crossroads before Greer was chartered. The family held a reunion in 1914 pictured here.*

the month. By the beginning of 1907, Greer's "swapping day" had moved to the second Monday. Jockey Day remained a part of Greer's tradition until progress crimped it around 1912. Construction of the interurban electric railway by James Buchanan Duke took the lines through the upper part of the city square. The trading location moved to a site on Mosteller Street where it thrived until it was banned from the city limits on January 9, 1934.

From the 1880s, general stores were two stories, containing upstairs rooms that were often used for public purposes. W.A. Hill had opened a spare room to both school and church. By the 1890s, Noah Cannon, H.P. Moore, and D.D. Davenport had constructed business locations that contained additional rooms to be used as halls for public meetings. Although they were called "opera houses," there is no record of an operatic performance per se in Greer's early years, with the exception of musical excerpts presented at music club meeting. These second-story halls did offer room enough for public educational meetings, professional conventions, and presentations by traveling shows, which offered comedy skits and literary readings. Rolla Ryan, "the Southern Comedian," entertained on April Fool's Day, 1882. Edison's Electrical Theatre and Specialty Company performed at Davenport's Hall on Saturday night, October 26, 1901. Admission was 10¢ and 25¢. The next year in January, Professor Meehaus's Dog and Monkey Theatre Company performed in Greer. On September 2, 1902, Lloyd and Genter presented "The Girl from Cuba" at Davenport's Opera House, charging 25¢, 35¢, and 50¢ for seats.

The facilities available in Greer prompted meetings of religious and professional bodies as well. The Enoree Presbytery met in Greer the week of October 4, 1902. Delegates from outlying areas too far to commute daily boarded with local church members. Frank Dixon spoke on January 16, 1907 on "The Man against the Mass" as part of the Lyceum series scheduled for Greer. The final presentation of the season was the Swiss Bell-ringers scheduled for April 2. Chautauqua shows also visited the town to bring entertainment and culture.

While the opera house revues appealed more to the educated and affluent, the circus and carnivals appealed to all. Fall and spring were carnival seasons. When the John R. Smith Show appeared in Greer in early April 1910, the streets were congested. Krause Greater Shows boasted ten acts, including a Ferris wheel and a merry-go-round, and appeared in October the same year. The feature attraction was Carter, the high dive artist who plunged into a tank of burning liquid. Central States Shows set up on the Hendrix lot on Trade during the week of April 5, 1918. The circus was a larger affair, requiring more space than available on the town square or a spare lot of the mill village. The George King property, at what now is the Peach Tree Plaza, was a popular location for circuses into the 1950s. Minstrel and medicine shows also visited Greer.

Another form of socialization was the annual reunion of the survivors of the Civil War. When the Greenville County veterans of Hampton's Legion met on July 5, 1875, Cunningham Pennington and John Greer were among those who attended. It is not surprising that communities assumed the duty and privilege of remembering the sacrifices of their fathers, brothers, and sons. The atmosphere of these commemorations was not one of defiant anger, but rather nostalgia, loss, and reconciliation. At Greer on June 25, 1886, Professor Kennedy's high school closed out the school term with commencement activities commemorating the Confederacy. The *Enterprise and Mountaineer* of June 30, 1886 reported the following:

> The most noteworthy part of the program was the rendition of the "Bonnie Blue Flag" by eleven young ladies, representing the eleven seceding states in the order in which they formed themselves into the South Confederacy. The singing was beautiful but I don't expect we should say anything about it, for if our Radical friends up north should hear of it they would raise a terrible howl. It was almost as big a thing as Jeff Davis' reception and, if it should go north, some of our friends up there would, very likely, become alarmed for fear that Greer's was going out of the union.

By the 1890s, Confederate veterans' reunions became more widespread as aging soldiers considered their mortality and their families desired to perpetuate their memories. Chapters of Confederate Veterans' organizations proliferated, as did other similar organizations created by the descendents of veterans. Company reunions were not uncommon. The most active such group in the Greer area

*CONFEDERATE REUNION. A reunion of Greenville County's Confederate veterans was held in Greer in August 1907. Almost 900 veterans and guests filled the town. Before they left town, veterans lined up across Trade Street in front of Wood-Mendenhall's Carriage Company. Photographer Charles W. Drace captured the moment.*

was Company F, 16th South Carolina Regiment. Reunions were held at Brushy Creek Baptist Church, a half-mile from the muster ground where the company had assembled in 1861 to debark for war. W.P. Taylor presided over the reunion of summer 1905 when about 20 people gathered for a dinner. Horace L. King, one of Greer's first schoolmasters, read reminiscences and anecdotes for the program.

In 1890, the United Confederate Veterans organized and, just three years later, had 255 camps across the South. On June 9, 1893, Camp Pulliam, honoring a Butler Guard killed at Gettysburg, was organized in Greenville. Colonel S.C. Crittenden was asked to organize camps at Travelers Rest and Greer. Confederate veterans in the Greer area had been meeting for a number of years at Brushy Creek Baptist Church for the surviving members of Holtzclaw's Company. Camp Joe Walker was the Greer camp of the United Confederate Veterans chapter 1291, which was led by W.P. Taylor and Captain John G. Greer. In the summer of 1910, Bertie Smith was elected sponsor and Nellie Abbott was maid of honor.

Confederate Memorial Day ceremonies had been held each year at the Greers High School Auditorium since the school was built. Beginning in the second decade of the century, the Daughters of the Confederacy assumed many of the duties in connection with planning and executing reunions, celebrations, memorials services, and meals to honor the aging veterans and remember the dead. The Hampton-Lee Chapter of the United Daughters of the Confederacy (UDC) was organized on April 23, 1910 with Mrs. W.M. Ballenger as president. By 1920, the Benjamin Brockman Chapter of the Children of the Confederacy completed the list of memorial organizations in Greer. Of the various organizations, the UDC was most vigilant, remembering each reunion day with meals and banners and occasionally taking a stand on public issues.

The UDC held their first Reunion Day in Greer for the "boys of the sixties" under the large oaks on the lawn of Simeon Hughes, one of the veterans and a former prisoner of war. In 1911, there was interest in erecting a Confederate Monument at Arlington Heights. The children of the local school raised $4.40. With insufficient funds, the project remained stalled for many years. In 1923, the UDC sponsored a play for the public to raise money for a monument to Greer soldiers of the Civil War, Spanish-American War, and World War I. Melba Murray and John Oliver Kendrick starred in the production "Microbe of Love." Girls served cold lemonade as a male quartet sang "the old songs." For reasons unknown, the monument was never installed. The Arlington Heights property was sold in July 1924 for use as a site for a new African-American public school.

Black citizens of Greer also had their fraternal organizations for socialization. By 1897, Greer had an African-American chapter of the Odd Fellows. Twenty years later, there were chapters of the Knights of Pythias Lodge 166 and Eureka Masonic Lodge 59.

*BERTIE SMITH. The Hampton-Lee Chapter of the United Daughters of the Confederacy, Greer, was founded in 1910. Miss Bertie Smith, one of the founders, served many terms as president through 1930. In 1915, she was elected vice-president of the state chapter.*

In terms of race relations, Greer's record has been mixed, as would be expected of any southern town. Among the earliest settlers who arrived in the area after the Revolution was a group of a dozen or so families from the slopes of Virginia. Along with the Cunninghams, Hammetts, and others were the McGlothlins, a family of free black mulattos led by James McGlothlin, a blacksmith-wheelwright. As the population grew, more blacks arrived, but the number of free blacks remained small. The earliest and most common relationship between the races was that of slave and owner. There were fewer slave owners in the upstate than in the middle and coastal areas. Most landowners, like Phillip Lester, had between four and ten slaves at a time. Hugh Bailey, with 20 slaves, was placed in the planter class.

African-American citizens figured importantly in the building of Greer. During the Jim Crow era (1890–1965), they were restricted by custom and law to menial and marginal work in town and at the mills. Despite the segregation, there was considerable diversity of occupational choices open for African-American men. In addition to farming (three levels: owner, renter, or cropper), there were jobs as driver, laborer, plasterer, janitor, barber, mason, painter, porter, carpenter, boiler man, and railroad worker. Professional jobs were teacher, preacher, and undertaker.

Successful black men also operated their own businesses beside their white counterparts. Around 1914, Luther Miller and Enoch B. Foster were partners in Star Pressing Club, a dry cleaning firm located in the old People's Bank building on Trade Street. Mitchell H. Thompson, a self-employed tailor, also located on Trade Street. The location of these businesses suggests an integrated clientele, since black businesses catering to black patrons usually located only within the black residential community. Considering the fact that Thompson was in competition with at least one white tailor, he must have been very skilled and successful.

African-American women who worked outside the home were most often employed as maids, household or restaurant cooks, or laundresses. Because black women had fewer occupational choices than men, they sometimes did manual labor when nothing else was available. The women moved dirt at the site of the construction of Apalache Dam in 1904.

The only professional work open to African-American women was teaching. In the black communities in School District 9, only one-fourth of the children had reasonable access to education under the segregated community school system. Beginning at the turn of the century and continuing for 20 years, Greer's black public school was Maple Swamp School located in Spartanburg County. Florence Hutchings, a white teacher, taught there in 1902.

One of the most ambitious projects undertaken in turn-of-the-century Greer was a private school for African-American children. The trustees of the North Enoree River Baptist Association acquired 8 acres on the east side of Greer in 1903 for a little over $300. The trustees, drawn from 15 area churches (one per church), included W.J. Foster, president of People's Undertaking Company in Wellford and member of Piney Grove Baptist Church. Foster, along with J.J.

Chaney, Lee Mitchum, and J.E. Sims, borrowed $575 three years later to construct a schoolhouse. By 1922, there were boys' and girls' dormitories on the site. Since W.R. Bailey had sold the land to the trustees, the school was called Bailey View and operated until December 1925 when creditors began foreclosure proceedings.

An exception to the Jim Crow rule, at least temporarily, existed in the domain of religious practice. Respect and friendship across class and racial lines was not uncommon. Slaves attended and joined churches with their masters' families. Brushy Creek Baptist Church recorded African-American members through August 21, 1867, when all were dismissed to form their own congregation. While blacks and whites founded separate schools, enjoyed separate recreations, and lived and worked apart in the decades after the Civil War, the one area where they remained close was that of religious faith. Revival times were customarily shared with whites visiting black churches and vice versa. Once inside the church, the seating was separate. The arrival of the Pentecostal Holiness Movement created a dilemma that forced citizens to confront their attitudes on race.

A revival at Double Springs resulted in the establishment of the first Pentecostal church in the area, Gum Springs Pentecostal Holiness Church. The Pentecostal church in Greer was a black congregation that had accepted the doctrine of the Holy Fire, an interpretation of baptism of the spirit adopted at a national convention in Anderson in 1898. L. Jackson Green, owner of Greer Lumber Company and a Confederate soldier, became the church sponsor. By 1906, he had sold a lot near the county line to the church for $100. The members gave Green six notes of $100 each to pay for the construction of the church by Greer Lumber Company. E. Dallie Green, his son and company manager, supervised the building project.

From the beginning, the Pentecostal denomination was integrated and remained so for over a decade. Although the Greer church had a predominantly black membership, a few whites, some devout and others curious, attended. Among the whites in regular attendance was L.J. Green. Because his attendance proved controversial, he endured criticism both from the public and some of his family.

On May 1, 1908, in Anderson, South Carolina, the Fire Baptized churches decided to segregate the church because of mounting racial prejudice. The Reverend W.E. Fuller, a black minister from Abbeville County, led the organization of the Fire Baptized Church of the Americas at the Greer church in November of that year, forming the organizational framework for black worshipers. Despite the segregation of the devout, L.J. Green continued to attend services in the black church that he had built until near the end of his life.

In Greer, segregation evolved slowly in other areas such as housing. By 1915, four African-American communities existed: Needmore, Slabtown, Maple Creek, and Greentown. The first three were located outside the town limits, roughly on the west, east, and south sides of Greer. Greentown, named unofficially for L. Jackson Green, was on the east with the Fire Baptized Holiness Church as its center. As Greer grew with the mill expansion, the need for housing increased for all classes and races.

One of the earlier residential areas was Mountain View Heights, developed in 1907 by Thomas Keating and D.O. Leonard on the condition that no lot would be sold to "any person of African descent" upon the penalty of the reversion of title. Ten years later, on the eve of World War I, the Beasley Addition for Colored People was laid out on the Walter DeShields property and consisted of tiny tracts of about 2,500 square feet.

Increased housing for black and white residents produced a need for better schools. At the turn of the century, the state of public education in Greer was at a low point. The mill village schools outside of Greer often had more superior offerings than those schools in town. A 1919 report from the Commissioner of Agriculture, Commerce, and Industries stated that while the public schools paid their teachers $60 per month, the Victor Mill and the Greer Manufacturing paid their teachers $100. It stated, "The best school buildings in South Carolina are in the mill communities."

On March 16, 1903, the county boards of education of Greenville and Spartanburg created a joint school district, the Greenville County segment continued to be designated as District 9-H and the Spartanburg County portion as District 79. A new school was built over the next year and a half. In 1905, J.M. Moore became Greer's first administrator titled superintendent of city schools, serving in dual capacity as superintendent and building principal. W.H. Cale, who followed Moore in 1910, was replaced by H.B. Dominick. When Dominick became superintendent, Greer had a Class C School, which meant that it had a three-year curriculum, offered ten units of credit, and had two teachers who held 40-minute classes for 36 weeks.

As the town grew, so did its student population. The new school that had served so well in 1905 was overcrowded within five years. Growing enrollment, primarily in grades one through six, forced the trustees to find classroom space in town. The upstairs room of the building on the southeast corner of Hill and Mosteller, known as the Company Store, was used for classes even after additions were added to the graded school. Local contractor J.C. Cunningham was contracted to construct four additional classrooms.

Since the 1880s, a high level of academic competency of graduates had been a tradition at Greers High School. Continuing with their education, some students excelled, as did Dr. Benjamin Few's son, W. Preston Few, who had risen in his profession to become dean of Trinity College (later known as Duke University). Two girls won gold medals in music competition at Greenville Female College in 1912; Charles Kendrick, class of 1916, won a four-year scholarship to Clemson, one of three awarded to Greers High School students. Marion Crowe, Greers High School, Class of 1914, became a teacher at Brushy Creek. At the Greenville County School Fair held in Greenville April 17, 1914, Greer only won three points, but they were in academic subjects, coming in third in math and second in recitation with no athletic competitors. Lois James Ratterree evaluated Greer's educational offerings many years later: "We were as well prepared [upon graduation] as anyone. As a matter of fact,

*GREER GRADED SCHOOL. Completed in time for the fall term, 1905, the school was outpaced by Greer's school population in a little over a decade.*

when I went to Winthrop in 1915, I repeated several subjects I had had at the Greer School."

By 1920, Greer's Graded School was again overcrowded. Classes were held in upstairs rooms over Trade Street businesses for several years while a new high school was being planned. Part of the crowding came from growth, part from compulsory attendance mandated in 1919. A part of the estate of D.D. Davenport, who died in 1918, provided half the funding for a new school, which was completed in 1922 at Moore's Heights (West Church Street) and named D.D. Davenport High School in his honor.

School crowding and population increase were a direct result of the building of more textile mills in the new century. William Burgess, forced to leave the presidency of Victor Manufacturing, returned to cotton mill enterprise in less than three years. In early 1900, he was looking for investors. While Franklin Mill was still in the planning stage, Greenville leaders tried to persuade Burgess to locate it there. Franklin Mill organizers wanted a spur line for freight, and the railroad had so far refused. Greenville leaders assured the mill men that such a spur could be had at Greenville and that land prices were much more reasonable than in Greer.

When property belonging to Emma Westmoreland, wife of organizer Dr. H.V. Westmoreland, became available, the matter of real estate was eliminated. W.W. Burgess (president), H.V. Westmoreland, J.D. Ashmore, J.H. Wyatt, E.C. Bailey, W.E. Waldrop, John Robinson, and L.A. Green chartered the Franklin Mills on September 17, 1900 with capital of $45,000.

*FRANKLIN MILL. A much smaller operation than Victor Manufacturing, it was located on the west side of town. Franklin was founded by William W. Burgess and others in 1900.*

Thomas Keating, a Greer contractor hired to build the first cottages for the mill hands, built the first 25 houses in the same style as those in Victor village. Each cottage had a kitchen and three rooms with ceilings only in the two front rooms. They were weather-boarded with unfinished lumber. The contract called for Franklin Mill to furnish the lumber and Keating to be paid $40 per house. Completion was set for December 1.

In summer 1900, construction on the mill began and it started operation in February of the next year. Initially, it was a yarn mill designed to produce only coarse yarns, operating on 5,000 spindles. A reservoir constructed behind the mill supplied the water for the boiler to power the steam engine. After a smooth start, stockholders increased capital investment to $60,000. Burgess remained until March 1902 when he left for a similar position at Fingerville. W.R. Tattersall, an Irish-American from Maine, was his successor.

The mills adjacent to town brought in hundreds of new citizens, mostly fresh from the rural and mountain areas. While most of the mill hands lived in the mill villages and traded with the company stores, they also brought considerable business to Greer, creating a boom time. Apalache Mill, variously known as South Tyger, Cedar Hill, and Arlington, grew as a mill community with its completion in 1904. While smaller than Victor, Apalache was thoroughly modern in its complement of machinery and experienced mill personnel.

While the mills supplied cottages for a majority of operatives, Greer experienced a building boom greater than anything it had yet seen. In this economic context, a building and loan association was formed. On May 7, 1906, B.M. Hughes, A.H. Miller, and H.B. Carlisle chartered the Citizens Building and Loan Association with $50,000 capitalization, raised by selling 50,000 shares at $1 each. The capitalization tripled to $150,000 in April 1916. The offices were located in the Bank of Greers.

In 1906, L.G. Miller, A.H. Miller, M.M. Bruce—all of whom were citizens of Greer—and W.T. Sauratt of Union organized the Planters Savings Bank. On Monday morning, January 14, 1907, J.C. Cunningham began work on the triangular building designed by Thomas Keating for the fork of Hill and Trade Streets. H.B. Carlisle was the president and, after two years, the bank had deposits of $23,000. In 1921, architects Beacham and LeGrand of Greenville designed a new building for the same location. The unusual triangular building cost $40,000 and still stands today.

In 1909, John Robinson, former boy telegrapher, investor, and supervisor at Apalache Mill, organized a group of local investors to build yet another cotton mill near town. By early 1910, Greer Manufacturing Company was operating and bringing more residents to town. Greer's fourth financial institution, the Peoples

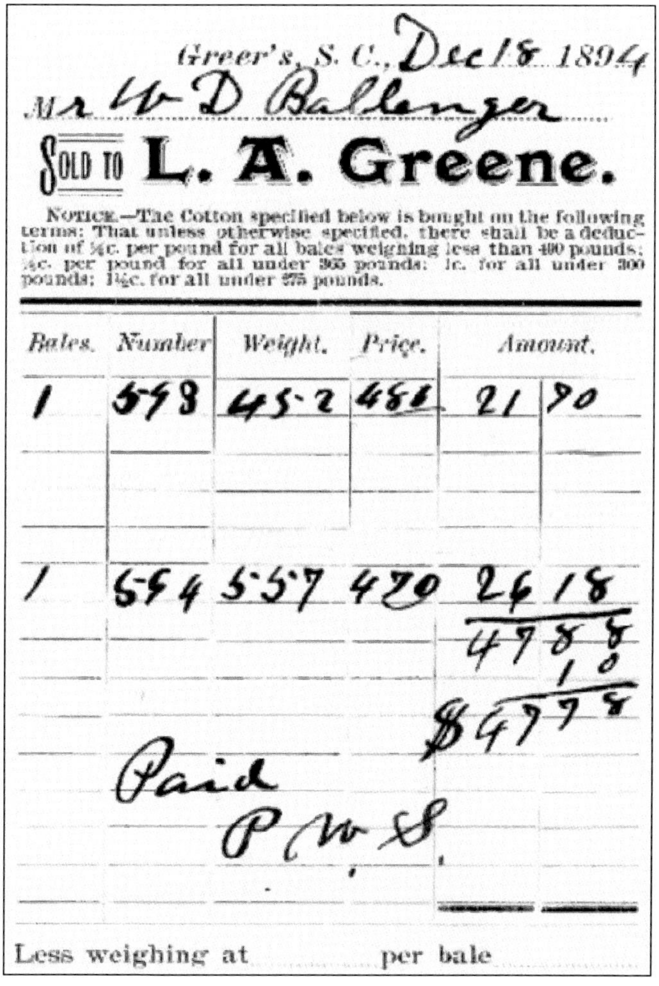
Greer's, S. C., Dec 18 1894
Mr W D Ballenger

SOLD TO L. A. Greene.

NOTICE.—The Cotton specified below is bought on the following terms: That unless otherwise specified, there shall be a deduction of ¼c. per pound for all bales weighing less than 400 pounds; ½c. per pound for all under 365 pounds; 1c. for all under 300 pounds; 1½c. for all under 275 pounds.

| Bales. | Number | Weight. | Price. | Amount. |
|---|---|---|---|---|
| 1 | 548 | 452 | 4 8/8 | 21 90 |
| 1 | 554 | 557 | 4 7/8 | 26 18 |
| | | | | 47 88 |
| | | | | 10 |
| | | | | $47 78 |

Paid
P W S

Less weighing at per bale

*L.A. GREEN COTTON RECEIPT. L.A. Green bought cotton in Greer almost from the beginning of the market. In 1900, he joined W.W. Burgess and others in establishing Greer's second cotton mill.*

Bank, was organized in 1910 in response to a booming local economy fueled by the cotton mill business. The bank was capitalized at $25,000 and opened in November in a two-story building on the Green lot at the corner of Trade and Main. Francis Inglesby, general manager of the Apalache Mill, agreed to be president, but resigned before the bank opened. Dr. Fred James replaced him and served as chief executive until 1913. Five years later, Greer's three banks had combined assets of over $1.5 million.

During the second decade of the century, banks did not address the fundamental farm problem, cash flow. Crop mortgages could and did cost farmers their lands. The government created the Federal Land Bank to funnel funds into the hands of farmers who were good risks and had unencumbered lands. The Farm Loan Association created local agencies to administer the funds. By 1917, three local associations, including Pleasant Grove National Farm Loan Association, were operating in Greenville County.

In 1920, J.B. Mendenhall, a local cottonseed and fertilizer dealer, and his partners W.E. James, W.L. James, W.T. Brockman, and Allen R. Hawkins, organized the fourth bank in Greer. C.L. Cobb came from Rock Hill to manage the Farmers Bank and Trust that operated until late 1923.

While nineteenth-century Greer was a town full of general merchandise stores catering to the farm trade, the next century saw the nature of business downtown change. Replacing general stores were shops offering groceries, meats, candies, and clothing. Service businesses such as livery stables, smithies, laundries, and

*APALACHE MILL. Apalache Mill was the final incarnation of a long time cotton manufacturing operation located on a site 2 miles from Greer on the South Tyger River. Apalache was a project of Victor Mill president Lewis Parker.*

*GREER MANUFACTURING. Greer Manufacturing Company, founded by John Robinson, was completed in early 1910.*

undertakers moved into town. By the beginning of 1905, Greer businessmen organized the Greer Board of Trade. One of its first actions was to petition the governor to schedule a special election to determine if Greer could become the seat of a new county. By January 17, 1907, 16 members of the board had signed the constitution of the organization whose stated purpose was to attract businesses that would specifically encourage the further development of Greer. At that time, the board was negotiating with an unnamed businessman regarding the construction of a laundry and ice plant.

Problems with the county line no doubt encouraged the movement to make Greer the seat of a new county to be called Highland. A plot of 100 square miles, including Victor, Apalache, Duncan, Reidville, and Holly Springs, would be designated for the new county. Leaders in the movement included J. Terry Wood, Malcolm C. Davenport, and T.E. Smith. Confidence ran so high during the campaign that people were sure that John D. Wood and Malcolm Davenport would be the new county commissioners. The vote on the issue was scheduled for fall. Thaddeus T. Westmoreland, again running for mayor, campaigned on this simple platform, according to the *Greer Observer*: "I am a candidate for mayor of Greer on a platform of equal rights to all, special privileges to none; stay sober, keep going. Hog in town if you want him."

Not only did Westmoreland lose, the county issue was defeated when citizens went to the polls on November 13, 1907. The *Greer Observer* commented, "Men may keep this town from growing." Actually, the opposite was true. Its neighbors took this small town more seriously. The *Greenville Enterprise and Mountaineer* began to refer to Greer as a "city" in most references after that.

While the new county did not materialize, the progressive outlook permeated the thinking of local businessmen and the Greer Civil League was formed in 1914. The Civil League's first agenda included plans for a fair when weather permitted. The next year, 27 young business and professional men formed the Cosmos Club to develop commercial, industrial, and moral interests.

One of the most important changes in early twentieth-century Greer was the arrival of a second railway. In 1909, a railroad company was formed to serve the growing commuter traffic and short haul freight in the upstate. The new electric railroad was not envisioned to replace the Southern but to complement it. This company would link cities of Anderson, Greenwood, Greenville, and Spartanburg to Charlotte and was known as the Greenville, Spartanburg & Anderson Railway (GS&A). The project to be created in segments offered some choice for the Greenville-Spartanburg link. Two routes were surveyed: the southern route ran through Reidville and Pelham; the northern ran through Greer and Taylors. On June 8, 1911, Reidville leaders met with officials of the railway and presented an impressive argument for the southern route. A petition bearing the names of every landowner on the route allowed the committee to bind themselves to a promise of a free right of way the entire 30 miles if the Reidville Route were selected. The Reidville route was also the shorter, and hence, less costly of the two.

The gift of the town square by William Shumate in 1882 posed a problem on the Greer route. Shumate had designated that the property could be used for construction of public buildings, but the proposed route of the GS&A would pass through the upper half of the property just south of the town hall and jail. The city council voted an easement to allow the route. To test the action of the council, E.C. Bailey brought suit against Greer and W.T. Shumate, hoping to give the council's action the force of a court order in determining the town's right to decide the best use of the Shumate gift.

Some outsiders did not believe Greer residents were as enthusiastic as the promoters of the Reidville Route. Any doubts about enthusiasm were allayed when the supporters of the Greer route provided a free public banquet at Chick Springs in honor of GS&A executives on May 29, 1912. The day before the barbeque, supporters announced the meal would be preceded by a 25-vehicle caravan from Spartanburg. The lobbying effort at Chick Springs resulted in no commitment from officials of the railroad. The track was being laid rapidly, having been completed for 43 miles toward Greenville. All lands were secure for the Reidville route, but several hitches remained in acquiring rights of way on the Greer route.

With Judge George E. Prince presiding, the Court of Common Pleas heard the case of E.C. Bailey versus W.T. Shumate, *et al.*, on June 12. The case was decided in favor of Bailey, that the town square could indeed be used by the railroad, but with certain provisions. A deed granting provisional right of way to the GS&A Railway was prepared July 3. The company, in exchange for a strip of 120 feet

*P&N DEPOT. The Greenville, Spartanburg and Anderson Railway Company (GS&A) was organized in 1909 to link the towns by modern electric passenger train service. Variously called the GS&A and Interurban, it became the Piedmont and Northern (P&N) Railway. Shown is the Greer Depot completed in late 1913.*

across the square, agreed to construct an adequate depot with office space for use by the town.

The directors of the GS&A heard the final arguments from proponents of both routes on June 13. J. Wright Nash, a Spartanburg attorney, presented the Reidville argument. The route was already clear of legal encumbrances and passed through farm and forest land that annually produced 16,000 bales of cotton and 530 cars of lumber. Pelham and Fairmont promised to expand if the lower route were chosen. Reidville, rich in minerals, would build a $100,000 brick factory. The Greer delegation, led by Dr. H.R. Black and Reverend Wardlaw, presented a simpler case that the railroad would pass where textile mills were located if the upper route were taken.

After the presentations, the directors adopted the Greer route, contingent upon securing the remaining rights of way. Once those were obtained, the track laying proceeded through Greer for the P&N Railroad, popularly called "the poor and needy." In fall 1913, a two-story brick depot was completed as well as a warehouse near the depot.

The P&N was successful from the beginning. It handled considerable passenger traffic from its opening run on March 23, 1914. A sleeping car was on order and the railroad company expected it to be available by the end of May. By mid-July, the Interurban, as it was called, had 14 trains passing daily through Greer. J.P. King was agent and Alex Mitchell assistant agent. Operating much

*P&N DEPOT, LATER VIEW. The P&N provided cheap passenger service, hence the popular designation, the "poor and needy."*

like a trolley, it made more frequent stops to accommodate passengers. After stopping at the depot, the train halted if passengers were waiting at Parker's stop near the edge of Franklin village and at King's stop near the Buncombe Road Crossing. At these stops were shelters with three sides and a top to protect passengers from the weather.

Greer's experience with the progressive spirit helped to prepare its people for the events of 1917 and 1918. The world had been at war since 1914, and Greer had already been briefly touched by European events when cotton was temporarily proscribed early in the war. From early 1915, war had brought increased prosperity to cotton farmers, buyers, and mill personnel. Despite President Wilson's hope for peace, war came to America in 1917 and Greer people responded.

# 5. Patriotic Greer: 1917–1920

World War I affected Greer long before local men began to volunteer for service or answer the call of Uncle Sam. The international cotton market fell into immediate decline upon the outbreak of war. For a time, cotton, because of its potential use in the manufacture of munitions, was considered contraband. Until cotton's status as a legitimate commodity was reestablished, farmers faced the threat of failure and struggled to shore up their credit with local merchants. Never before had local farmers directly experienced the pressures of international market forces. Once the issue was settled among the warring nations, cotton prices rebounded within months, and prices exceeded the wildest dreams of farmers who had witnessed the bottoming out of cotton during the mid-1890s.

Escalating tensions between the United States and Germany made war almost a certainty and excited the spirit of adventure in the minds of some young men who had listened to the war tales of their grandfathers. Town fathers and local members of the UDC organized a citywide, patriotic observance on May 10, 1917, a little over a month after war was declared on Germany. Graves of Confederate veterans were decorated during the morning; special services were held at the Methodist church with Presbyterian and Baptist ministers participating. A community-wide parade was held at 4 p.m. with mounted police, city officials, fraternal orders, members of the UDC, young recruits about to disembark for training, and members of the community at large marching in support of the "war to end all wars."

When the United States entered the war in spring 1917, a draft was instituted to fill the ranks of the military. Draft registration was held at Greer on June 5, 1917 for men over 21 and under 35. The Greenville County Registration Board completed initial tabulation of available men on June 6. Approximately two-thirds of the young men aged 21 to 30 in the country who registered claimed exemption. In Greer, 121 white men claimed exemption and 71 did not. Among African Americans, 23 claimed exemption and 56 did not. At Greer Mill, only 9 men of 65 claimed exemption. Although many men from Greer claimed exemption initially, only a handful actively dodged the draft.

Men who served received public recognition. The Greer Drug Company displayed photographs of 50 local boys who had entered service. The First Baptist

Church honored its 12 members who were in the armed forces by special services and prayer. The tide of patriotism ran high in Greer. In 1916, Thomas L. Smith and M.D. James, two young businessmen who had opened a haberdashery at 222 Trade Street, felt compelled to answer the call of their country. Specializing in men's business attire, they had operated the store for almost two years when they closed shop in late summer 1918 and sold their stock of goods at cost to enlist in the army. Even at that time, predictions were that the war could last several more months, but the German's will to fight deteriorated, the Kaiser fled to Holland, and the war ended in November. Smith and James returned to reopen their store on March 1, 1919. Smith & James, which operated continuously thereafter, survived the deaths of the original partners and today remains one of the oldest businesses in Greer.

Training camps were established at Greenville for the 118th Infantry (Camp Sevier) and Spartanburg for the 117th Infantry (Camp Wadsworth). Located on the main passageway between the camps, Greer saw the passage of perhaps thousands of soldiers arriving and departing via the Southern Railroad and the P&N. The community attracted many of the men to churches, sporting events, and local service organizations, which provided entertainment and a taste of home for homesick soldiers. A friendly rivalry between these camps and the special location of Greer made the town a popular leave site. A number of Greer men were assigned to the 118th and frequently visited families, brought friends, and participated in the social life of Greer. Ballgames were popular in the spring and summer of 1918. On April 5, the two camps met on neutral ground at Victor Ball Field where the 118th beat the 117th by a final score of seven to one. Greer

*CAMP SEVIER 118TH INFANTRY COMPANY. Camp Sevier, a training camp located between Greer and Greenville during World War I, temporarily housed a number of Greer soldiers. Shown is a camping area reserved for a company of the 118th Infantry Company.*

*CAMP WADSWORTH. A World War I training camp located in Spartanburg, Camp Wadsworth was a friendly rival with Camp Sevier in leisure time activities such as baseball games, which were often held on the neutral grounds of Victor Mill ball park at Greer.*

extended hospitality to soldiers in other ways. Mrs. W.A. Peahuff opened her home as temporary quarters for the families of Lieutenant J.A. Morgan and Captain J.W. Swann, who wanted to be near the officers before they shipped out. Other residents followed suit as citizens and soldiers made acquaintance with one another, locals often inviting an officer or enlisted man to partake of Sunday dinner or spend a weekend. Sometimes long-term friendships evolved from these simple acts of kindness. In some instances, more than friendships developed as several young Greer women met their future husbands at local events sponsored for the benefit of service men.

When Camp Sevier was first populated, entertainment was lacking. C.W. Drace, photographer and proprietor of the Grand Theater, arranged to have a tent assigned as the camp theater in 1917 and showed silent movies until the Army began providing the same entertainment. The military recognized the value of movies as a morale booster and eventually operated 36 "Liberty" theaters in as many training camps.

Men from Greer known to have served in the military during World War I and returned include one of the first men from Greer to enlist in the army, Harold K. James, son of Dr. F.G. James. Those who served in the military are listed below:

| | | |
|---|---|---|
| Anderson, James H. | Hawkins, Harper | Suddeth, Croel |
| Arms, Archie L. | Holtzclaw, Boyce | Thompson, Walter P. |
| Barker, Ben W. | Holtzclaw, James M. | Turrentine, Samuel A. |
| Black, S.D. | Howell, Bunyon | Vaughn, Guy Wayman |

| | | |
|---|---|---|
| Black, Theron | James, Harold K. | Wakefield, Herman |
| Brown, Ed | McCall, James | Wakefield, Roy |
| Collins, Roy | McCarter, Fred | Walker, Morris Kennerly |
| Dill, Ernest T. | McKown, Horace | Walker, Theron O. |
| Gilreath, John H. | Paris, Carl | Wilson, Herman |
| Gilreath, P.D. | Robinson, John A. | Wood, Oliver |
| Green, L.J. | Smith, T.D. | Wood, William E. |
| Groves, Hollie A. | Smith, William Bailey | Wright, Herbert |

Some such as John Gilreath, who served in the Quartermaster Corps at Fort Moultrie, never left the states. Eventually, some 5,000 men enlisted from Greenville County during the world war and 89 died; 14 and possibly as many as 17 were local men. At least two others from Greer died from wounds shortly after returning from overseas.

Those who died in combat in France included Private Tandy Hawkins and George Hart, a Victor Mill worker. Grady G. Davis of the 323rd Infantry and Minlo Mathis of the Sixth Regiment, United States Marines, also died in France and were buried there. Two local soldiers returned to Greer severely wounded and died within months. Bissell Littlejohn, 21, died of his wounds in 1920 after suffering for almost two years from gas in the Argonne Forest. Miles Prilow Howell, son of J.L. Howell, died on September 7, 1921, at 28.

*CAMP WADSWORTH DITCHING DETAIL. "You'll never get rich, digging a ditch," but these soldiers in this ditching detail had to make the dig to guarantee good drainage in wet weather.*

*WALTER ALVIS CLARK III, WORLD WAR I SOLDIER. Son of a cotton mill carpenter and grandson of a Confederate veteran, Walter Alvis Clark served in the Infantry and saw action in France.*

As in virtually all wars before the discovery of antibiotics, many died not of bullets but of disease. John Johnson of Franklin Mill village died in May 1918 in New York. Ben Odam, adopted son of evangelist Dean Crain, died aboard ship returning from the war and was buried at sea. Citizens of Greer, led by Reverend Porter Bailes, created a scholarship in Odam's memory. The scholarship provided $100 through Greer School District for a student to attend North Greenville Academy. The wounded often returned permanently afflicted. Luther Hester and Jim Miller were both disabled by mustard gas while fighting in France. Five African-American soldiers from Greer died while serving: Simpson Cohen, Woner Dean, Abraham Dixon, Jime Leatherwood, and Luther McMakin. After the war with Germany ended, a brother-in-law of the Reverend Porter Bailes was killed during the Russian conflict.

Men from Greer who performed heroic deeds beyond the normal call of duty included Melvin N. Hardin who received the Distinguished Service Cross for extraordinary heroism near Bellicort, France, the last days of September 1918. Hardin, the company runner, had according to his citation exposed himself time and again to shell and machine gun fire, "showing absolute disregard for

*ALONZO BEACHAM, WORLD WAR I SOLDIER. Alonzo Beacham served in the Infantry in France after joining the army in 1917. He trained at Camp Sevier before his departure.*

personal safety" while maintaining communications between combat units. Private William Edward Wood, Company E, 118th, received the same award for "extraordinary heroism" near La Selle River in France on October 17, 1918. Armed with a Lewis gun against a German machine gun emplacement, he led a squad of men and drove the Germans from their position. Wood's squad continued to push the enemy back even after their own position was hit by shellfire and their Lewis gun destroyed.

The most decorated Greer veteran was Private Edgar Osborne McDowell who, at 19 years of age, was awarded the British Military Medal by the Prince of Wales on November 22, 1919. McDowell, an orphan from the mountains, came to Greer to live with relatives on a mill village near Greer. After enlisting in the army, he was assigned to the 118th Division, Company F, the old First South Carolina regiment. On October 8 at Montbrehain, France, after being severely wounded and with his right arm badly damaged, he single-handedly rushed two machine gun nests that were firing on the rear of his company. He killed and captured a total of 26 Germans, ending the threat of those two positions. A number of Germans surrendered to McDowell, who then delivered his prisoners to the rear before seeking medical aid for himself. He was also awarded the French Croix de Guerre with gilt star and the Distinguished Service Cross. An act of Congress of March 2, 1929 provided mothers and widows of soldiers interred in Europe the opportunity to make a pilgrimage to their loved one's grave. Lillie Mathis, mother of Minlo Mathis, and Alice Davis, mother of Grady Davis, requested the opportunity to make the trip and visited their sons' graves at St. Mihiel, France.

Once war began, Greer citizens united on the home front. Rumors abounded from the coast to the foothills regarding German spies. Fear of espionage resulted in guards being posted at the railroad bridges between Westminster and Duncan. Support for the war effort came in diverse forms. The young women of Victor Mill village formed a patriotic league. Churches held prayer meetings. James L. Brown headed a chapter of the United War Workers, which held patriotic meetings and raised money to provide soldiers with small necessities and magazines. Local businesses sponsored the war effort by promoting the sale of war bonds, contributing to war-related funds and charities, and holding jobs for men who enlisted in the military. The Bank of Greers sent out patriotic greeting cards to its customers. The United States Employment Service of the Department of Labor selected one man from each school district to serve on a Labor Board, which would report any shortages of help due to the draft. They also reported idlers who were not contributing to the war effort. E.C. Bailey represented Greer. Manning Dillard, Dr. R.F. McKown, L.A. Green, John Rollins, J.L. Howell, A.J. Farnham, and I.F. Few represented rural areas surrounding Greer.

Greer supported the war effort with cash as well. During America's participation, four Liberty Loan Drives were held to raise money to support the war. John Robinson, cotton mill founder and realtor, was chairman of the Greer District during the third drive. At a three-day rally held at the graded school on April 15 to April 17, citizens heard speeches and songs and were encouraged to buy a bond. As the war neared its final days, the Fourth Liberty Loan campaign began in Greer on Monday, September 30, at the town hall where $15,000 was subscribed at the meeting. A measure of Greer's patriotic spirit can be appreciated in that the amount raised in two weeks was enough to have capitalized another cotton mill, "going over the top," pledging $182,900, almost $14,000 above the quota.

Greer residents also supported the war effort by growing vegetable gardens and conserving goods and commodities in short supply. The National War Garden Commission encouraged everyone who could to grow vegetables for personal consumption. Small gardens sprouted on most residential lots throughout Greer in the spring of 1918. This was the first war to emphasize the importance of food supplies as a resource for winning. Dr. W.T. Brockman was appointed Captain of Food Conservation with six lieutenants to assist him. The Reverend M.H.

Thompson organized support among the local African-American citizens. A food conservation meeting was held on November 2, 1917.

For area farmers, the 1918 season was problematic. War demand drove prices of farm products up, because certain chemicals used in agriculture were also used in making munitions. The federal government rationed fertilizers for the planting season of 1918. Shipments that began arriving in Greer in April 1918 were designated for wheat crops only. Cotton fertilizers were supplied later. Even cotton farmers in Greer benefited from the high demand produced by the war. In turn, the mills ran full shifts to provide cloth, canvas, and gauze, as well as clothing and sheeting, needed for the military. Mill hands and owners prospered, the latter of whom saw the stock value of cotton mills rise to unprecedented highs. Victor-Monaghan stock soared 16 percent in the three weeks ending March 13, 1918.

Farmers were also hard-pressed to find enough seasonal help to plant, work, and harvest crops. By 1918, Selective Service had taken a toll of those usually available for temporary farm work, and the harvest was gathered largely by the schoolchildren of the county. When the labor shortage became acute for farmers that summer, most of the schools instituted summer sessions beginning in July to permit children to work on the farms in the fall. In Greer, the largest fall crop was cotton, an estimated 12,000 bales grown in the outlying communities.

The rapid population growth in the Greenville-Greer-Spartanburg area brought with it the likelihood of epidemic in a pre-antibiotic era. The Spanish Flu arrived in Greer during the late summer and early fall of 1918. Unlike any outbreak of the flu most people had experienced, this strain of the disease claimed lives even of the young and vigorous. Flu-like symptoms appeared and worsened

*DIVISION HEADQUARTERS, CAMP SEVIER.*

*STANYARD PEARSON, VETERAN AND LIBERTY HILL FARMER. Pearson, an infantryman in the war, returned to the farm near Liberty Hill community and trucked produce by wagon from his farm to sell in Greer. He is shown here in his carriage in 1919, a prosperous farmer perhaps on a weekend outing.*

as the disease ran its course; more than anything else, it resembled the pneumonic plagues of the past. The skin turned bluish, the lungs filled with fluids, and fever and fatigue depleted the body. No one was immune; crowds and assemblies were a source of transmission.

After a carnival on Friday and Saturday, October 4 and October 5, 1918, near Greer Mill village, 100 of the village's 600 residents became ill. At Victor, there were only six cases reported at the same time out of a village population of almost twice that of Greer. Military bases were particularly vulnerable. Sloan Burnette died at Camp Jackson on October 7. The State Board of Health declared a quarantine the same day for Greenville city and county; under penalty of law, all assemblies including school, church meetings, and entertainment were prohibited. At Greer, the school board voted to suspend school for up to ten days. The city council prohibited public entertainment or gatherings until further notice, including church and social affairs. As the disease continued to spread, the quarantine was extended. Greer schools and mill schools remained closed into the second week of November.

Part of Greer's preparedness program included the organization of a chapter of the Red Cross. Mrs. E.H. Shanklin, wife of the Franklin Mill superintendent, was president. By May 1918, the chapter had over 300 members. Meetings were held in the auditorium of the graded school. One of the early projects of the local chapter was to gather linens to supply Belgians displaced by the German invasion. After the arrival of Spanish Flu, the local chapter began collecting money to buy bed sheets for Camp Sevier where the disease was epidemic. Most local farmers, when solicited, donated a pound of cotton or its value in cash for every bale sold on Tuesday, October 15, 1918.

When the "flu" arrived in Greer, local doctors were overwhelmed with the surge in their caseloads. Greer physicians had patients scattered over large practices extending from the country to the mill villages and the city itself. As the disease loosened its hold on Camp Sevier, available medics were assigned to work with Greer doctors for several weeks to help provide necessary care to stricken civilians. The state lifted the county quarantine at midnight on November 1, but Greer remained closed, as did the mill villages. Only the Victor YMCA remained open, providing certain necessary services for mill hands.

News of the truce created a holiday in Greer. It also marked the first public gathering since the arrival of the Spanish Flu. The guns in France fell silent at 11 a.m. on Monday, November 11, 1918. All businesses closed or never opened that morning as virtually everybody celebrated in honor of the war's end. Streets were packed; automobiles were decorated in flags and bunting; church bells rang; and mill and fire whistles blew.

The quarantine continued through November. Each passing train brought with it the threat of further infection. A Chatauqua program scheduled for November 23 was cancelled, but three of the performers, soprano soloist Clara Watkins, her accompanist Althea Reffelbower, and reader Lucy Pennington, arrived without knowing of the quarantine. They remained overnight at the Smith Hotel and gave a program for fellow guests.

The lessons of World War I were not lost on the citizen-soldiers who formed National Guard units around the country. In November 1919, James W. Wood and Julius F. Miller organized a local unit made up of veterans. One of the first National Guard Units in the state, it was under the command of Captain James W. Wood, a textile worker who had served 18 months in the army during the war. Once the guard completed certain government requirements, it received federal recognition on June 6, 1921. By August it had 65 members. When it was inspected for the first time on August 16, it had just received its rifles. Colonel Fred R. Day of Columbia inspected the group led by Captain Wood and First Lieutenant Lonnie Winstead.

Patriotic feeling ran high in Greer during the years following the war. The Great War, as it was known, was especially important to southerners. Participation in a war over ideals completed the re-unification of the North and South, yet the arrival of the Armistice was no guarantee of permanent peace. The Russian Revolutionaries threatened further conflict. In this context, the National Guard at Greer and elsewhere readied themselves for any eventuality. The camaraderie and pride of those terrible months of world war were not easily relinquished. Greer, because of its central location between major towns in two counties, hosted a sham battle in May 1922 with guard units from Greenville, Spartanburg,

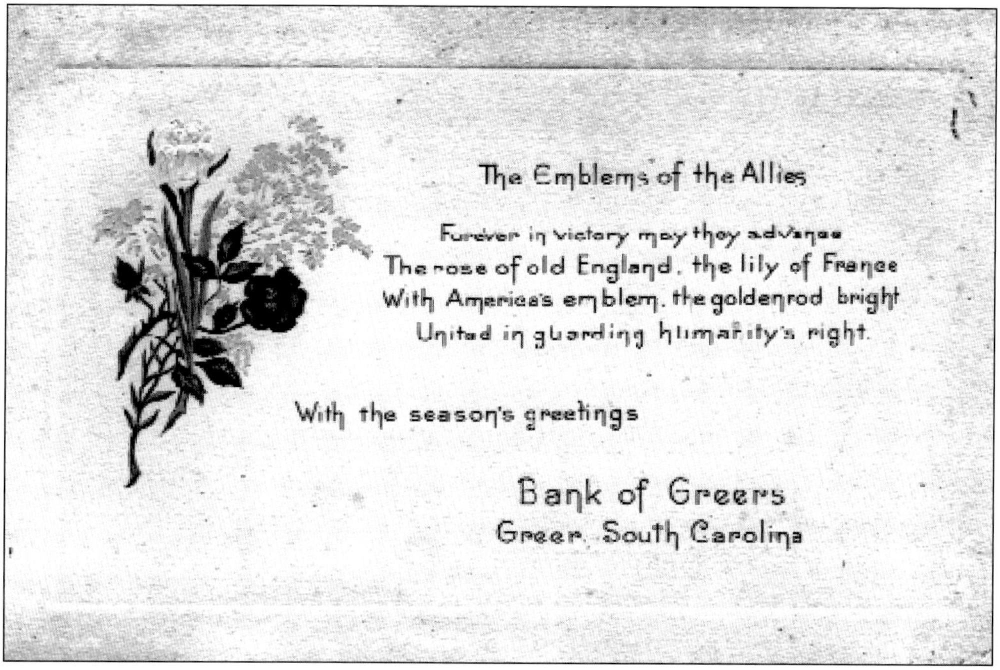


*CHRISTMAS CARD, 1917. Greer flew the colors high during the First World War. Virtually everyone was involved in an effort to support America's position. The Bank of Greers sent its customers patriotic Christmas cards in December 1917, as shown here.*

Easley, and Union engaging in war games just outside of town with camp on the Victor ball field. The two-day event was a holiday for Greer as soldiers, police, bands, and dignitaries marched down Emma Street to the campsite. Speeches by the mayors of Greer, Easley, and Union and a public barbecue prefaced the sham battle. The battle involved roughly 20 percent of the guard then organized in the state.

The National Guard retained a permanent spot in Greer. Originally organized as a howitzer or field artillery company, it underwent reorganization just before World War II. The first armory was located between the P&N and Southern Railroads on School Street. A new armory with additional garage facilities was constructed on Cannon Street during the late Depression.

# 6. The Tumultuous 1920s

The arrival of the 1920s promised a new wave of prosperity for Greer. Most of the men who had gone to serve their country had returned safely after the Armistice. Greer, except for growth, had remained unchanged. Still a cotton town, thousands of bales per season made their way to the cotton yards beside the Southern Depot. Five cotton mills shipped products from and received freight at Greer. Three mill supply houses, two cotton gins, a resident cotton broker, and several seasonal buyers rounded out the influence of the most important commerce in town. A population of 2,000, combined with hundreds more at the mill villages, kept busy the more than 100 retailers. Into the 1920s, practically everyone owned a radio and hardware merchant William Thompson did a steady business selling automobiles. New banking facilities, schools, and church structures complemented the prosperity of commercial Greer.

The county line issue surfaced again in 1920. The National Highway between Greenville and Greer had been completed in the summer of 1918, but two years later, the roads north and south remained rutted, rocky, and at times impassable. The Greer Apalache Road was critical to the delivery of coal and food to the mill village. Even though local citizens offered to bear half the cost, Spartanburg County refused to repair the road. The solution, as seen by Greer leaders, was to petition to have the legislature place Greer in one county only; Greer opted for Greenville County. Speeches and debates highlighted a bitter campaign filled with name calling. When it was over, Greer lost by a handful of votes and remained straddling the county line. Despite the hard feelings, the fight actually had a positive effect. County officials from Greenville and Spartanburg promised to fulfill their obligations. In January 1923, Greer officials hosted a banquet for both county delegations to thank them for the paving and to plan how best to deal with local issues.

With cotton prices in decline at the end of the war, Greer also had to face the prospect of competitive cotton markets in other nearby towns. In this economic context, Greer merchants formed the first chamber of commerce. In January 1920, a membership campaign was conducted that raised $5,000. In May, Henry W. Link, managing editor of the *Spartanburg Evening Herald*, became the full-time secretary. During the next two years, the chamber, located in a small frame building on Emma, focused on improvements designed to make Greer more attractive to business, such as better roads, improved health services, and better electrical service. The chamber also advised farmers and sponsored educational programs to introduce alternative agricultural products. Link worked closely with cotton buyer T.E. Smith to promote Greer as a farmer's town. By 1925, the chamber disbanded. Competition among merchants selling essentially similar lines apparently sharpened. While overall business remained generally prosperous, the mid-1920s were marked by what was politely called "non-cooperation" among merchants. This lack of business unity and self-interest prevented the revival of the chamber. In a front-page editorial, the editor of *The Greer Citizen* asked the following:

> How do the merchants of Greer differ from those of surrounding cities? Is something wrong with the town or the merchants? We know of no better place to live in the world than Greer, so it must be the merchants. One is afraid the other fellow will get an inch on him. Many of them knock each other instead of telling the truth, that is that good merchandise of all kinds can be found in Greer.

The chamber building became the Greer Public Library on November 18, 1925. Seeing the need for a free public library, the Civitan Club funded it until January 1, 1926 when it became the first branch of the Greenville Library. Mrs. E.R. Minus, librarian, and Mrs. Joe Buford, assistant, registered 1,171 borrowers the first year.

SOUTHERN DEPOT. *The Southern Depot was completed in 1910, the Southern Railroad Company representing consolidation of several small rail companies like the Airline, which created the need for the town of Greer.*

*GREER OFFICERS IN 1927. Undermanned and confounded by Greer's location straddling a county line, officers had to rely on aid from both county sheriff's departments and occasionally special officers sworn in for specific duties. Shown are Officers Charlie Liverett and W.L. Flynn.*

The successes of the 1920s brought a time of fundamental transition to Greer. The first challenge was the postwar decline in cotton prices. Caught off guard by falling prices, a group of investors had committed to build a second cotton warehouse. Among the investors in Greer Bonded Warehouse Company was Chaney Littlefield, buyer and cotton dealer for almost 30 years. At the time of the warehouse construction, cotton traders were enjoying a time of strong demand for their commodity. Through June 1920, cotton had remained at around 40¢ per pound. By September, it had declined somewhat more, selling for 35¢ a pound. Prices of most consumer goods plummeted as merchants tried to attract business. Cotton prices continued to drop through much of the year. W.R. Gray, assistant county agent, estimated 40,000 bales were made in the county, yet little of it had surfaced on the market. On October 4, cotton was at 25¢ a pound at Greer. Three weeks later, cotton traded at Greer for 21.5¢, a half-cent lower than the Greenville price.

Around breakfast time on November 19, 1920, Littlefield, who had invested heavily in the cotton market when prices were higher, placed a pistol to his temple. Bank president and brother of the chief of police, Littlefield had held his cotton, anticipating a price of 50¢ a pound. He had borrowed heavily to invest. Misjudging the price peak, he lost close to $10,000. Its continued decline plunged him deeper into debt. Less than three hours after firing the fatal shot, Littlefield died. Other cotton brokers lost money as well, but most weathered the drop in prices and continued to fuel Greer's commerce.

Closely allied with cotton farming and textiles was banking. The decline of cotton prices, arrival of the boll weevil, and the uncertainty of cotton manufacturing ushered in changes in local banking. In late 1921, Peoples Bank had become the First National Bank of Greer, opening accounts with several important local stores, including Stone & McKinney and Hobbs-Henderson. In early 1923, the Bank of Greers and Farmers Bank and Trust agreed to merge. The new corporation, Greer Bank and Trust, was capitalized at $100,000 with a $50,000 surplus. To the deal, Farmers Bank and Trust brought customers of a building and loan association it had established, as well as ownership of the cotton warehouse on the public square. Organizers were E.C. Bailey, Allen Hawkins, T.E. Smith, and W.E. James. E.C. Bailey served as president, and Cobb and B.A. Bennett were vice-presidents. As with the Farmers Bank and Trust Company, Allen Hawkins was cashier. John Ratterree of York headed the insurance department of the bank. In late winter 1924, the bank moved to the corner of Trade and Victoria.

The last banking institution organized in Greer prior to the Great Depression was Greer Agricultural Loan Association, established in 1927 by E.C. "Ece" Bailey, R.H. Bearden, and R.M. Hughes. Organizers planned to deal in farm loans, specifically notes made by farmers to the Federal Intermediate Credit Bank of Columbia, but they cancelled their charter in December 1928.

By 1920, the average farmer was either a tenant or well on his way to becoming one. Farming had been in decline, especially in the Cotton Belt. Unable to influence markets, except by withholding products until the prices were highest, farmers were sorely in need of warehousing facilities at reasonable prices. Two such facilities were built at Greer about the same time. Greer merchant Mendenhall and cotton broker Louie James built a warehouse in the 300 block of Trade Street, between the depots of the Southern and P&N Railroads. Farmers Bank and Trust, which financed the project, held title after merging with the Bank of Greers. A second warehouse, Greer Bonded Warehouse Company, located on Depot Street on a lot formerly owned by Greer Fertilizer Company, was chartered on August 17, 1920. The principals were J.E. Gibson, J.D. Ashmore, and Chaney Littlefield. The building was small but modern in the protection it offered cotton stored there. It sat apart from nearby structures and had an automatic sprinkling system, a feature missing in many similar and smaller warehouses without access to a city water supply. John A. Robinson, a principal in two Greer cotton mill starts, was elected president.

Warehousing did little to help farmers other than to preserve the quality of their product. Cotton prices fluctuated around the break-even value to farmers, forcing tillers of the soil to try innovative organization, such as cooperative marketing. This system cost Greer some business, sending farmers with their cotton to larger cities. The Greer Chamber of Commerce, led by president T.E. Smith and H.W. Link, secretary, reacted in an effort to keep the cotton business in Greer. The chamber selected as its goals for the year 1922 "the establishment of industries which will help farmers find ready markets for their produce and the combating of the boll weevil." Greer merchants, however, held little hope for traditional cotton farming as a viable twentieth-century enterprise. The chamber encouraged crop diversification by arranging for local cotton farmers to visit Hodges, South Carolina and Catawba County, North Carolina to investigate potato and creamery operations as alternatives to cotton production. By 1927, cotton trade in Greer had peaked.

Greer farmers did diversify their crops and began to specialize in garden produce, apples, and dairy operations. A few attempted to grow apples, while some farmers became dealers in mules and plow horses. The crop of choice, however, grown by many of the farmers who abandoned or reduced cotton production, was peaches. Peaches had been grown in the area for family use and on a small scale since the earliest settlement. Phillip Crymes Lester had the first peach orchard of record in the Greer area. During the 1820s, he raised peaches and apples at Pleasant Grove. While the extent of Lester's orchard is unknown, it was tended during an era before crops could be transported to larger markets.

W.A. Pollard and James P. Taylor were early peach pioneers. Pollard had a small orchard that he maintained while serving as Greer's postmaster. Taylor had a farm on the outskirts of the town. According to family tradition, his 5-acre orchard was in production in 1898. Taylor has been called the "father of peach growing in South Carolina." According to one tradition, Taylor shipped the first boxcar of peaches from Burgess Stop in 1912. State records and news accounts, however, suggest the Greer area commercial crop was insignificant before the middle teens. The larger producers were J.V. Smith and W.W. Burgess, who planted commercial orchards north of town early in the twentieth century. While Burgess's interests and energy were more diverse and eventually focused upon an extremely successful career in real estate, Smith became the town's most active full-time peach grower about 1913.

The Piedmont was especially suitable for peach growing because of favorable soil, plentiful rainfall, and good climatic conditions. The two railroads offered access to a northern clientele. Peach growing was not, by any means, as attractive as cotton farming, because of its cost in trees and fertilizers, its pest problems and orchard maintenance, and the wait from planting to harvest. Farmers who planted peaches were landowners and investors, a more prosperous and stable class of farmer than the typical cotton grower.

Burgess, Taylor, and Smith all owned orchards in close proximity to one another north and west of Greer. Taken together, their efforts were highly significant in promoting agricultural diversity to Greer-area farmers. Smith was undoubtedly the region's foremost promoter of peach production. Farmers desiring to make a change apprenticed themselves to him, learning the trade from Smith who was free with advice based on his own experience. Palmer Dillard, an early student of Smith, learned grading and marketing from Smith in exchange for the use of Dillard's gasoline tractor, one of the first in Greer, to plow his orchard. Dillard said the following:

*PACKING HOUSE, MT. VERNON ORCHARD. The peach packing house at Mt. Vernon Orchard in 1914 was owned by J. Verne Smith, Sr. Smith was the area's foremost promoter of peach production and gave freely of his knowledge to fellow farmers.*

> Verne didn't have a tractor. [When I was plowing for him] He wouldn't let me go home for dinner. He took me to his house. When the orchard needed plowing, I drove it up there in the early morning and left it. I walked home each day until the plowing was done.

After leaving Clemson to run the family farm, Dillard planted his first orchard in 1923 and picked his first crop three years later. He began with 5,000 Elberta peach trees.

In 1917, Earle Taylor, son of J.P. Taylor, began his own orchard, planting 30 acres. The younger Taylor, along with his brothers, had learned techniques from J. Verne Smith, working part-time for him when they were not in school. Earl Taylor began with 2,000 trees and experimented with several varieties. He marketed his crop locally at first, hauling wagonloads to Greenville, and later trucking them to Asheville and Hendersonville. After Taylor hauled crates of peaches to North Carolina where they brought a healthy return on his investment, he began to ship peaches by rail to northern markets in 1920.

*TAYLORS PEACH SHED. Earl Taylor, son of J.P. Taylor, began to work peaches in his own right at age 18 in 1917, planting 30 acres in peach trees. Prior to this time, he and his brothers had worked for J. Verne Smith, learning the trade. Shown is Taylor's packing shed.*

By that year, Smith's orchard had developed into the largest and most profitable in the state. The 35-acre orchard produced 20 boxcars of peaches at a profit of $1,000 per car during the 1920 season. About this time, Smith bought another orchard in Alto, Georgia and divided his time between the two farms. Smith's enterprise became a model for area growers. In September 1921, some 60 peach growers met at the J. Verne Smith Orchard. Greer Chamber of Commerce chairman H.W. Link welcomed them. From this meeting grew a marketing organization uniting Piedmont growers. By 1924, the South Carolina Peach Growers Association was formed to market peaches on a model similar to the cooperative system that was succeeding with other crops. Earle R. Taylor and Verne Smith were elected delegates from Greenville County to a meeting in Columbia on March 12. Greenville County had 60,000 trees, about 10 percent of the state's total. Smith was elected director of the South Carolina Peach Growers Association in early 1924. By 1926, the Greenville County crop stood at 100,000 bushels.

Greenville County had the jump on Spartanburg as peach country by over a decade, but the lead did not determine the winner of the race. Ben Gramling had led the way when he and a group of Spartanburg County farmers met at Gramling's and agreed to plant 30 acres in peaches, Gramling himself planting one-third of those. Three years later, the first peaches were shipped from Spartanburg County. On the Spartanburg side of Greer, brothers R.A. and I.B. Dobson formed a partnership around 1925 and grew peaches as a part of a diverse farming enterprise known as Dobson Brothers Farms. Beginning with a few hundred trees, the Dobson orchard grew to 200 acres by 1976.

As an alternative or supplemental crop to cotton, peaches had much to commend them. Once in production, the orchard had similar cultivation and harvesting requirements and labor costs were about the same, but the potential profit was considerably greater than for cotton. Smith sold $15,406 worth of fruit from his 5,000-tree Greer orchard in 1926. The critical element for peaches was blossoming time as it took only a short exposure to subfreezing temperatures to kill the tiny peach. Cotton, on the other hand, could be replanted if disaster struck early in the planting season. The customary way of dealing with this threat of cold weather was to plant varieties that bloomed well beyond the latest anticipated freeze. The varieties of choice among Greer growers were the Elberta and the Belle of Georgia.

By the last of July 1931, J.V. Smith estimated he had shipped 25 railroad boxcars of peaches from his orchard. Smith had traditionally sent a box of peaches to the White House each season, starting with Woodrow Wilson's presidency. When asked if his tradition would continue in the midst of deepening economic crisis, Smith was noncommittal as to whether Herbert Hoover would get a crate of peaches from Greer. Peaches were the lowest they had been in years, selling at between 50¢ and 60¢ per bushel. Smith died in 1933 before he was able to renew his orchard through

*DOBSON BROTHERS. R.A. and I.B. Dobson formed a partnership during the 1920s that amounted to nothing less than Greer's earliest agri-business enterprise. The photo shows the brothers, I.B. on left, during grain harvest time about 1930.*

*GRAIN HARVEST. Farm hands harvest wheat on the Dobson Brothers farm* c. *1930. The Dobson brothers came to have one of the most prosperous peach farms in Greer.*

replacement planting. Smith's knowledge, gained through experience, created the foundation upon which later orchardists built Greer's last major crop as a farming town. Staggered planting, regular spraying, pruning, plowing, and testing new varieties, all had been learned by Smith through the "hands on" approach.

Spartanburg County producers gained considerable publicity over the next 20 years as South Carolina challenged Georgia for rights to the name "Peach State." In 1935, the Dobson orchard consisted of 2,600 trees and it more than doubled over the next decade. Dobson Brothers renewed their orchards in 1948 with 4,500 saplings. As peaches became increasingly important to the Greer area economy, Greer Peach Distributors, Inc. was organized by Abe and Alex Senter in the summer of 1945 to buy and ship local peaches. By 1948, the peach business was a $5-million industry in the state with 500-plus cars shipped, a significant portion of those coming from orchards surrounding Greer.

Peaches brought a new prosperity for Greer. By the end of the decade, a local abattoir and packinghouse operated by William Brown marketed meat products under the "Peachland" brand. Over the next decade, the police department and the Bank of Greer used the peach as a symbol of Greer enterprise. For nearly a decade beginning in the mid-1950s, the Greer Peach Festival brought a degree of even international recognition of a small town's accomplishment by promoting its agricultural base. Local promoters brought to Greer regional celebrities and dignitaries and at least one Hollywood star to help celebrate the peach harvest. President Lyndon Johnson and Queen Elizabeth II were sent silver medals commemorating the annual event at the height of its popularity.

The peach industry required considerable short-term labor for picking, grading, and packing for shipment as each crop came in. High school and college students primarily supplied the labor force. The Jones Brothers Cannery, which began operations during the declining phase of Greer's agricultural era, offered more jobs related to the peach industry. The cannery bought local peaches. Nor did peach culture lend itself to any of the non-owner-operated forms of farming. Even the larger orchards provided year round work for only a handful of men who plowed the orchards, fertilized, and pruned the trees as required. The final reality for farmers of Greer in the end of the twentieth century was that building lots were, as the real estate expert says, "the highest and best use" of the land.

While peaches grew on the hillsides just outside of Greer, the town was plagued with widespread vice as well as occasional serious crime. At the beginning of the

*DOCKWORKERS. Rick Jenkins and Roy Mills (front) and Robert Burnside (on porch) at Dobson's peach packing shed.*

1920s, Greer's population was about 2,500, a seven-fold increase in 30 years. In 1921, David Moore succeeded Police Chief Charlie Littlefield. The police department had increased from one to four officers. Despite Prohibition, whiskey flowed in greater abundance than ever, fueling other forms of lawlessness.

David R. "Dave" Moore came to Greer from Duncan to serve as chief of police in February 1922. Moore had applied to the town council for the job, promising to rid Greer of public drunkenness and eliminate the illegal whiskey trade. Moore presented information that he had gathered as a private citizen. He believed that he could develop sufficient evidence to convict several bootleggers known to supply Greer with whiskey. Convinced that his inside information could be effectively used, the town council appointed him. His contemporaries described Moore as a determined man possessed of physical courage.

Council passed a tougher vagrancy law in March to begin the new campaign. On February 21, 1922, Moore and two officers arrested William Adams, who was apparently drunk and disorderly. Adams, a big man, put two officers on the ground and was in the process of trying to take the pistol from one of the officers when Chief Moore struck him in the head with a nightstick. Adams's skull was fractured and he died from the blow. Moore's action, although justifiable, created controversy and may have impaired his effectiveness. A number of incidents, many of which were either out of his jurisdiction or beyond his power to prevent or control, left his position with the city council weakened. Moore's sources either dried up or became reluctant to testify.

*PEACH MEDAL. The Greer Peach Festival was commemorated by special collectible medals issued by the Greer Coin Club. Designed by J.L. Jones and Talmadge Crisson, they were sold and/or given away to promote Greer. The one shown was minted in 1967.*

To some extent, the violence of the 1920s was a characteristic of the times; other places suffered lawlessness. Still, for its size, Greer was a violent town. In addition to the constant problem of public drunkenness, serious incidents increased, keeping public focus on the effectiveness of the police department. Cases during Moore's tenure, not handled to the public's satisfaction, included the killing of a popular mill league baseball player and an unresolved suicide. The most sensational event during Moore's tenure was the case of Dorothy Dodson, 21, who died on October 26, 1924.

Dodson, a known prostitute and figure in several police cases, was found dead in a house a half-mile southeast of Greer on the National Highway (Old Highway 29). A bullet had pierced her temple; a gun was in her hand. Public consensus was that she had been killed by one of the two other people in the house at the time. Although out of Greer police jurisdiction, the case came to reflect badly upon the local department because it brought statewide notoriety to Greer.

When no one claimed the body, the victim was slated for a pauper's funeral. Instead, local merchants contributed to a fund and First Baptist Church minister Reverend Porter Marcellus Bailes, a graduate of Furman and Southern Baptist Theological Seminary, preached the funeral. Bailes, originally from Fort Mill, had arrived to preach at the First Baptist church in 1917. While his delivery was powerful, his sermons were about simple themes: sin and its consequences, morality, and the duties of the Christian. With Baptists far outnumbering other denominations, Bailes became a voice of conscience for Greer during a tenure that saw the church roll increase from 295 to 731. From his first months in Greer, Bailes took the lead against public immorality and never relented. He spoke at a mass meeting in October 1917, urging citizens to clean up the town. From then on, he was a leading voice in the effort to restore law and morality to Greer.

Bailes delivered one of his most powerful messages over the body of the prostitute. "Who Killed Dorothy Dodson?—What Sin Will Mean to You" was heard by an estimated 1,200 people who attended her funeral. Bailes blasted the authorities for failure to act in the case, jurisdictional questions notwithstanding. In Bailes's view, the facts established demanded a public moral outrage and immediate action. Compounding the matter, Agatha Plumbly, a minor, was reported kidnapped on November 11.

Concern over the matter reached the governor's office when W.H. Willimon, foreman of the Spartanburg County Grand Jury, requested a special state officer. Governor McLeod assigned State Constable W.W. Rogers to come to Greer and arrest suspected parties. Although there was public outcry for action, the case was never resolved to the satisfaction of Bailes and his supporters. Citizens were outraged over the Dodson and Plumbly cases, and complained to the city council. The next month, the council elected a new police chief, W.J. Tapp.

Tapp, who had been associated with the company store at Apalache at least since 1918, had risen to manager and lived on the Apalache Road. Described as a devoutly religious man, he played piano at church services. A man of strong convictions, a leader, and believer in fair law enforcement, Tapp was hired on

February 10, 1925. Under pressure to clean up Greer, the council, which retained the authority to hire and fire officers, retained only Officer Charlie F. Liverette from the previous police force. The police department reorganization in February 1925 included the following officers: Chief W.J. Tapp, Day Officer Liverette, and Night Officers J.G. Skinner and C.F. Davis. The next month, S.O. Mahaffey was sworn in as special officer.

Changes in the make up of the police department did not change the town. Both petty and whiskey-related crime persisted. On May 2, 1925, a passing crew of burglars robbed the safe at Belk-McKnight Company, escaping with $1,000. They were captured later in Tennessee. Allen J. Moore, arrested on a charge of drunkenness, hanged himself in August, becoming the first suicide recorded at the local jail. Reverend Porter Bailes, preaching unrelentingly on Greer's depravity, continued to focus on the Dodson case. He preached his "famous sermon" again on October 25, 1925, exploring the reasons for the death of Dorothy Dodson. Less than a year after Tapp was hired, on January 21, 1926, Reverend Porter Bailes compared Greer to Chicago. Speaking on Greer's underworld in his sermon, he cast Greer as a budding Chicago with its own mob-type culture. Before the next Sunday's sermon, as if to punctuate Baile's condemnation of Greer, a thief stole C.M. Ponder's car from the front of the Baptist church. It was the tenth car stolen in Greer in two months. At the time, police officers were still foot patrolmen.

Shortly after the Ponder incident, Bailes received a call to preach from the First Baptist Church in Lakeland, Florida. His second call in a month, Bailes accepted, and his congregation reluctantly bid him farewell. Before he left, the church gave Bailes the unheard of honor of conferring upon him the Doctor of Divinity degree for his work in Greer, an action questioned and scrutinized by scholars and Baptist leaders for years.

Despite the best efforts of the town council and the ministers, Greer continued to deal with what could not be construed as anything other than a crime wave. During the late 1920s, the level of crime continued unabated although most of it was of a minor nature against property and public morality. Robberies such as the break in of the Greer Armory on School Street in March 1927 were common. Clothing and 17 Colt Automatic pistols were taken. Dr. Thomas L. Justice and the deacons of the First Baptist church drew up resolutions against worldliness—drunkenness, immorality, card playing, and dancing—and mailed them out in February 1929. The bulletin notified members their fellowship was in jeopardy if they partook and persisted in these acts.

One evening in 1927, Chief Tapp took a call from a black cafe near the town limits where a man was threatening patrons and had driven most of them away. Upon entering the building, Tapp was confronted by an angry, drunk, black man named Adam Watson, who was armed with a knife. Tapp ordered the man to drop his knife and come out. Instead, Watson advanced on Tapp with the knife extended in a threatening manner; so, the chief drew his revolver and fired. Watson died of his wounds. Although Chief Tapp was cleared after a coroner's investigation ruled the killing justifiable homicide, he was deeply affected by having to take a man's life and was unable to immediately resume his duties as chief. S.O. Mahaffey temporarily replaced him. Tapp returned and continued to serve as chief, some of his doubts perhaps put to rest by unceasing criminal activity in the small town. Incidents such as a gunfight between Dupree Gilliam and Greer officers in early 1928 kept police busy. Gillam was wounded and sentenced to four years in prison.

Chief Tapp was reappointed throughout the Depression era. To some extent, Greer's reputation for lawlessness was a product of the many communities that made up the town but were not legally a part of the defined limits. By the 1920s the notion of "town limits" had little bearing on the reality of what constituted Greer. Mill and African-American communities were actually larger than the legally defined town of Greer in terms of population; and country folk for miles in all directions meant "Greer" when they told others they were "going to town." Irresponsible and excessive drinking, fistfights, cuttings, wife beating, child abuse, and assaults kept Greer officers busy. Crime outside the city limits was still

*CHIEF TAPP. Chief of Police W. J. Tapp served Greer from 1925 to 1941. Tapp was so traumatized by the necessary taking of a life that he had to take some time off duty afterwards.*

associated with Greer even when local authorities had no jurisdiction. The faces changed with time, but the trends of the 1930s mirrored those of the 1920s.

During the years the Ku Klux Klan was reorganizing, the Red Scare of the postwar period further encouraged its spread, eventually into all of the contiguous 48 states. This new version of the Klan, fueled only in part by old precepts, even invited African Americans to support its opposition to the immigration of Catholics and Jews. In the mid-1920s, the Knights of the Ku Klux Klan reached a peak membership. Its strength was in small-town America and was generally perceived by members and outsiders alike as another fraternal group, much like the Masons, Redmen, and Pythians.

The new Klan arrived in Greenville County in 1921. Greer was one of the first sites of Klan activity in the county when on June 28, 1923, 100 hooded men paraded through Greer. While Klan meetings were held in the Greer area, the organization did not have a home until 1926 when a meeting hall became available. Public rallies were held near the King property and the P&N Depot. A Klan parade in Greer on April 30, 1925 included state Klan officials, mounted Klansmen riding robed horses, and footmen.

The Greer organization, chartered in 1926, constructed a building with business offices located on the ground floor and a large meeting hall on the second floor. The incorporators and officers consisted of what many would consider the "better class" of men, including large-scale farmers, lawyers, bankers,

*KU KLUX KLAN MEDALLION. This identification medal was carried by Klan members during the 1920s. The Greer Klan was a relatively small presence.*

and other businessmen. The Greer Klan thrived for a year with much pomposity and ceremony, but not much more. An upstate convention of Klans met in Greer on May 18, 1927. A parade, led by members of the Greer Police Force mounted on horseback, climaxed the day's meeting. The Pelzer Band furnished the music. Notably absent from the day's events was a cross burning. Instead, the local organization elected new members as well as delegates to the state meeting.

For a brief moment in Greer's history, the Klan maintained both visibility and a degree of respectability. Joe Hop, a Chinese laundryman who operated a business from 1924 to 1928, washed, starched, and pressed the robes of Klansmen, and set them in his windows. The starched helmets stood alone with empty eyes glaring at passersby, silently conveying a sense of security to some, a warning to others. A scandal in 1927 within the National Klan leadership helped to bring an end to the popularity of the organization. Membership dropped dramatically and suddenly as the leading citizens hoped to dissociate themselves from what they mistakenly had joined.

Greer meetings were most often lecture/discussion sessions and occasionally included brief sermons conducted by invited clergymen. Patriotic observance was an important component of the program, including the presentation of and oath of allegiance to the American flag and the recognition of veterans of the world war. Perceived threats of the Jew and the Catholic were discussed at least as often as was the race issue. Part of the ritual was alms giving. The Klan tried to maintain an alliance with the Protestant church. A single Klansman appeared at Concord Methodist Church during services in November 1927 when world war veterans were being honored. He silently made his way to the altar where he deposited an envelope containing a donation, then left the church quickly to a car waiting outside. The visibility of the local Klan declined dramatically after 1927. Although no public meetings are known after 1931, Klan presence in the Greer area, however, persisted beyond the 1930s. Even then, its numbers and influence were small.

Despite the problems of a tumultuous decade beset by new anxieties and problems, Greer continued to progress in significant ways. The concern for public health begun in the last century continued. In 1922, the town board of health, consisting of Dr. T.O. Walker, James L. Brown, banker Belton A. Bennett, druggist L.B. Johnson, George Garrett, and policeman Charlie Liverette, took steps to remedy a lack of public health services available to most citizens of Greenville and Spartanburg Counties. The population of the Greer area outside the town limits was large enough to require public health services from Greer rather than from either of the two county seats since most Greer residents had no transportation. Greenville and Spartanburg legislative delegates worked in mid-1923 to establish a Greer Health Zone that included Greer, Greer Mill Village, Victor Mill Village, and adjacent areas containing 7,500 people. Dr. J. Harvey Venning was supervisor. Hardly any imaginable area involving prevention, diagnosis, or health education escaped his notice. Schoolchildren were vaccinated and evaluated, wells were inspected, and literature was distributed. The only area not directly under Venning's control was meat inspection, which was conducted by local veterinarian Dr. N.J. Ayers, who was appointed meat inspector by the town council in 1925. In 1932, a hospital built at Taylors at the old Chick Springs Hotel cut the distance by half for Greer emergency cases.

During the 1920s, education at Greer was exciting and progressive, literally and figuratively. H.B. Dominick resigned under pressure. W.H. Ward of Fort Mill, who succeeded him, introduced the Gary Plan of Work-Study-Play, the first known adoption of this method in a southern school. Ward wanted to utilize existing classroom space more efficiently. Traditionalists opposed the Gary Plan and progressive education that was a catch-all term for experimental techniques. Essentially, the plan amounted to little more than the creation of study halls. He hired a gymnasium-playground teacher and an auditorium teacher. During the school day that ran from 8:30 a.m. to 4 p.m., with the noon hour for dinner, large groups of students left the classroom to these areas for study and activities. Ward presided over the first senior class to be held over en mass for another year in 1921 when an 11th grade was added to the district schedule.

At the end of the 1922–1923 session, Ward resigned. Edmund Wroe, a native of Kentucky and graduate of Chicago School of Law, took the Greer post that had more than 100 applicants for the job. Wroe, a progressive though not in the same sense as his predecessor, established night classes at the high school by the beginning of 1924. Under Wroe's leadership, Greer students enjoyed field trips and the senior trip became a tradition. Earlier, Ward had developed agriculture classes that were continued. Girls now had a domestic science program. During

*FIRST GREER HIGH SCHOOL BASKETBALL TEAM. It was organized in 1920 and was the first athletic team organized for competitive sports at Greer High.*

*LAST SENIOR CLASS: CENTRAL SCHOOL 1922. This photo shows the last senior class at Central School (formerly Greer Graded School), May 1922. The new Davenport Memorial High School was completed by the end of the school term.*

the 1920s, the mill schools became a part of the local school district. Bus service started for students at country schools at Pelham and Pleasant Grove, whose schools discontinued their high school courses.

When Edmund Wroe suffered an illness forcing his resignation, S.W. Rabb arrived in 1928 to superintend Greer schools. He continued the tradition of strong local education while fighting in the newspapers and in public against an early county school consolidation effort. Although operating near the limit of its fiscal potential, Greer School District did not fail to provide quality education for its pupils. Quality of education had been a major factor in the town's growth. In Fall 1928, the *Greenville News* published a list of 59 Greer High School graduates then attending 21 different colleges, representing a rate of more than 25 percent of the graduates.

# 7. Depression and War: 1929–1945

Two months after the collapse of business on Wall Street, crowds lined the streets from Ballinger's Store at the corner of Poinsett and Main down to the P&N Depot. Fifty decorated automobiles appeared for a Christmas parade that began at the Armory on School Street. Santa in one of the autos gave away hundreds of bags of candy to children along the route. Early the following year, local folk continued to attend the movie theatres made more exciting by the technology that brought the audio dimension to screen entertainment. The Grand Theater proudly announced, on February 6, 1930, that its first talking picture, *The Great Gabbro* starring Betty Compson, would be shown the following Monday.

Almost a year after the stock market crash, Greer was still growing; cotton continued to fuel much of its business, although the textile industry was continuing to weaken as a result of a decade of over-expansion. Most textile leaders, however, had no reason to doubt that demand would catch up with supply and reinvigorate the industry as it had in the past. Cotton manufacturing had reached a point at which further immediate expansion was counterproductive; too many of the new mills were involved in making similar products. Unsold cotton merchandise glutted the market. Through the mid-1920s, expansion had been viewed as a sign of economic health, but as wholesale demand dropped, mills cut wages, curtailed production, and brought in the newest labor-saving technology of the era in attempts to deal with the situation. Despite these and traditional remedies, the cotton textiles industry continued to decline during the late 1920s. Local mill stocks became less attractive to investors and sold at less than par value even before the 1929 crash.

Still, local investors who owned some mill stocks were not overly concerned about events on Wall Street in October. Collective wisdom dictated the economy would continue to boom and bust because the nature of the system was considered to be more a natural phenomenon, not within the province of human control. Prudent businessmen continued to invest in moderation, maintain a diversified portfolio, and remain ever alert to new opportunities for profit. They also always held something in reserve for times when the economy inevitably softened.

The banking industry had solidified Greer's reputation as a commercial and business center. By the beginning of World War I, a vigorous economy based on the cotton trade had given rise to four banking institutions in less than 20 years. The next 15 years saw local banking undergo even more radical change. In a sense, the banks of Greer were each economic indicators of change in the foundations of the general economy. Local banks were in competition for a limited amount of business; they were also dependent upon a farm product that fluctuated in value seasonally; and they were unprotected from the whims of large investors located states away who were not directly connected with local conditions. Local banks reorganized and consolidated until there were two, Planters Bank and Greer Bank and Trust Company.

The decade of the 1920s had seen the bases of the town's economy begin to erode. Farming and textiles simultaneously weakened. Cotton was a common link between the two. The farm problem rested on deeper underlying issues of long standing. The transition from subsistence farming to cash-crop dependency had cost over half the farmers in South Carolina title to the lands they tilled and, by the third decade of the century, many farmers were deeply mired in debt to the banks. The arrival of the boll weevil further endangered the traditional farmer's way of life. Farmers, who once persuaded cotton trading merchants to "carry them on the books" from year to year until a good harvest brought real profits, faced bankers who required better collateral than a promise or a hope. Defaults could and did bring foreclosure proceedings. Greer remained connected to the farm and the mill, in ways like two anchors, in other ways like two millstones.

When the crash of 1929 occurred, it had no immediate impact upon Greer. Despite being a New South town with a recent history of booming economy, Greer was still a part of the South, a region literally crushed by the war of the 1860s. Measured against the prosperity and promise of the North, the South and Greer remained backward in many ways: the local farmer was in debt, perhaps his lands mortgaged; the mill folk in the mill settlements around Greer could not depend upon the regularity of work and often owed the company store; and the merchants of Greer relied on these two communities for their own success. For most people in Greer, the days following the crash were ones of life as usual.

Some 11 months after the crash of the stock market, convinced that warehousing was a proper course for farmers facing weak markets, banker and longtime cotton buyer E.C. Bailey joined with banker B.A. Bennett in organizing Farmers Bonded Warehouse Company. The firm, chartered on September 8, 1930 and capitalized at $10,000, took over the warehouse business previously operated by Greer Bank and Trust Company. Organizers such as William B. Smith and W.E. James put up $2,000 in cash and raised the rest through the sale of gold bonds. The bonds, issued in denominations of $500, optimistically promised redemption after ten years to be paid in gold.

Optimism was somewhat premature. By July 1930, the assets of the local banks had shrunk 20 percent. With increasing withdrawals and ever-slackening business, both banks opted for ways to remain in business. Planters Bank tried to ride out the Depression by borrowing from the National Credit Corporation No. 6, predecessor to the Reconstruction Finance Corporation. Federal aid was minimal, however, and the depositors continued to withdraw funds. Greer Bank and Trust merged with Peoples State Bank of South Carolina, a banking chain with offices located around the state.

Despite the efforts of both banks, the funds were not there to maintain even a minimum daily business. R.M. Hughes, cashier at Greer Bank and Trust, supported the bank with his personal funds during its last days. Withdrawals overwhelmed deposits; Hughes's personal assets were depleted. Hughes had invested 25 years in the bank when it collapsed in late 1931. The conditions were much the same at Planter's Bank where steady withdrawals led to the bank's collapse on January 25, 1932. At the nadir of Depression, Greer citizens found themselves rather suddenly without a bank. Against this backdrop of economic failure and weak expectation, the most successful and longest-lived Greer bank was organized.

In December 1924, State Bank examiner Albert S. Fant announced that "grave irregularities" existed in the operations of the Bank of Duncan and the bank must close for audit. Greer investors E.D. Green, A.H. Miller, and L.G. Miller had organized the bank in 1909. Investigation of the matter eventually led to charges against L.G. Miller, a founder and former officer of the bank. Miller, who had been Spartanburg County treasurer, was convicted and sentenced to a prison term. The Bank of Duncan closed permanently and a new organization, the Peoples Bank of Duncan, opened early in 1925. Principals involved in the new banking enterprise included W.S. Glenn, president of the Carolina National Bank of Spartanburg; O.M. Moore, a Duncan merchant and planter; Alfred Moore, a cotton mill executive; and two Greer businessmen, Malcolm C. Davenport and J.C. Cunningham. Because of the integrity of its officers and banking practices, the Peoples Bank of Duncan was one of only three banks in the county permitted to remain open for business without restrictions after President Franklin Roosevelt initiated federal banking control.

Meanwhile, with Greer banks all having failed, local people were forced to travel to Duncan to do their banking business. Since Greer provided the bank with more business than did Duncan, the logic was clear as to the best location. Belton A. Bennett, M.C. Davenport, and others from Greer persuaded O.M. Moore, a major stockholder, to sell to Greer investors, who moved the bank to Greer and changed the name of the institution to Bank of Greer on June 16, 1933. By the next year, the Bank of Greer had assets of over $300,000.

When the Greer Bank and Trust Company failed, E.C. Bailey found himself in the cotton warehouse business full time. He leased additional building space and operated state bonded warehouses. By 1934, Farmers Bonded Warehouse Company required additional capital, but was unable to raise needed funds from investors. The corporation mortgaged five lots in the public square to J.C. Cunningham in 1934 for $10,000. By 1935, the United States Department of Agriculture instituted a policy of withholding recommendation of federal

*DEPRESSION DAYS CAR. Despite the Depression, James C. Howard admired his new car. Howard scraped up enough money to buy a new Ford in 1933. Ford provided train fare for Howard and other buyers to come to Detroit to pick up their cars at the factory.*

licensure of any building for use as a warehouse with a capacity of less than 1,000 bales. The Farmers Warehouse, estimated to hold between 500 and 600 bales, fell under the regulation. Anticipating reduction of business, the company reduced its capitalization in 1935 from $10,000 to $3,000.

Between 1930 and 1932, the effects of economic stagnation took hold on Greer. The 1930s brought much change in the way business was conducted with the greatest changes affecting the farmers. The New Deal regulation of farm products restricted farmers, first on a voluntary basis and later on a compulsory basis, in terms of what they could grow and how much. Cotton was regulated from farm to gin to factory. These regulations helped bring to a close the open-air cotton market at the lower end of town. Industrial plants nationwide were regulated in terms of wages and hours available to operatives. The textile mills in the Greer area slowly recovered. As the New Deal progressed, local government leaders learned how to apply for newly allocated federal funds for maintenance and building of school buildings, roads, and bridges. During the early stages of the

Depression, there were a few new start-ups, while most retrenched or held out for better times. Greer Drug Company decreased capitalization by 60 percent by 1936. C&D Chevrolet, organized by J.C. Cunningham and R.D. Dobson in 1927, decreased capitalization twice in 1934. Franklin Mills increased its capitalization in 1930, but shortly thereafter fell into receivership.

After 1932, the worst year of the Depression, business optimism returned. John Ratteree and Company continued to grow; D&D Motors became the successor to Thompson's Hardware as the local Ford dealer; and the Tire Exchange was organized. John Ratterree first sold insurance, going into business with W.M. Hawkins in early 1929. In 1934, he formed a company with A.C. Dawson. Ratterree weathered the Depression, became an underwriter in 1940, and organized the firm known as Dixie Fire and Casualty Company, which grew into Southern Home Insurance Company, a major company in the region. By 1960, capitalization of his company had grown from $300,000 to $2 million. In 1932, Vernon Duncan and Lloyd Hunt began the Tire Exchange. Hunt, a Pickens native, also invested in real estate during the Depression and reaped a fortune when the economy recovered.

*THOMPSON HARDWARE. William Thompson opened his hardware store in 1906 and within three years was Greer's first automobile dealer, shipping in Ford autos for customers who came from as far away as Easley, Jonesville, and Spartanburg.*

*DOBSON'S GIN. Dobson's Cotton Gin operated until the early 1980s when cotton was no longer a significant crop in the Greer area.*

To encourage trade during the worst days of the Depression, businessmen organized the Greer Merchant's Association in 1933. Sales, raffles, and giveaways were sponsored by the organization for several years. A typical example of the campaigns the organization promoted was that of the fall of 1937, when the association sponsored a raffle every Wednesday afternoon. For 11 weeks, winners would each receive $50 in the drawing. Member firms were encouraged to promote their own stores by having discount coupons offering special sales. About 60 percent of the merchants joined the organization and actively participated in its efforts.

Farmers Warehouse languished until 1939, when brothers and business partners R.A. and I.B. Dobson bought the warehouse. Combined with their facility on the National Highway (Old Highway 29), they had sufficient storage space to attract good business. They also offered the added services and products of their ginnery and fertilizer business in Spartanburg County. Sons of J.P. Dobson, who had established his farm as the largest and most valuable on the Spartanburg side of Greer some 35 years earlier, Dobson Brothers assumed the outstanding mortgage on Farmers Warehouse and paid $2,000 for the facility. The Dobsons hired W.E. James to manage the warehouse and buy cotton for them.

The war in Europe returned a degree of prosperity to Greer. Local mills contracted to manufacture military textiles and regular hours returned to the workforce. When war became a real prospect for the United States, the call-up of the National Guard followed months later by the draft, reduced Greer's industrial

*GREER MILL AND VICTORY TEXTILES (ORIGINALLY FRANKLIN MILL). During the war, the textile plants became part of the war production machine. Shown is Greer Plant where uniform twill and tent canvas were manufactured.*

population, opening for women job opportunities never before seen locally. The mills ran continuously to fill orders during the war, putting overtime wages into pockets of workers and in the Bank of Greer. By 1940, the assets of the Bank of Greer had climbed to over $1 million. Even then, the amount was less than half the asset base of pre-Depression Greer banks.

The difficulty of the Depression for Greer citizens lay in the fact that South Carolina was changing from an agricultural to an industrial state. By 1930, South Carolina had more people who lived in cities, towns, and settlements than on traditional farms. The nature of city and town life was one of ever-increasing dependency on a mill or factory, a "public job," or simply working for someone other than one's self. In earlier times, victims of the economy could always return to find refuge on the family farm. At the height of the Depression in Greer, the victims of job loss, hunger, and homelessness had to rely upon public support. Responding to the growing population of needy, the town created Greer Relief to aid helpless women and children and to eliminate house-to-house begging. The Greer Booster Club agreed to turn over its funds to the organization and undertaker John D. Wood offered free office space to administer the program.

After Mrs. O.T. Lawing was named to head its day-to-day operations, she planned a campaign to raise additional funds. By 1933, the national figures for unemployment reached 25 percent, and while Greer figures are not known, the local relief agency was apparently swamped. One of the federal government's programs involved transfer of surplus staples from warehouses to the needy. Free cloth, flour, and other necessities were given out from time to time at the local agency. By 1932, another agency was needed just to distribute the goods because of the number from surrounding areas seeking help. The local newspaper suggested, editorially, that a Red Cross Chapter be organized for the purpose; the Red Cross of World War I era had disbanded. Instead, local citizens opted to expand the work of Greer Relief. With a totally volunteer staff, it continued to operate and expand its work, eventually formally organizing with a charter in May 1936.

Immediate relief for the poorest of citizens was the first objective of the New Deal. Aimed at putting food on the tables of the needy and providing work for the jobless, the Works Progress Administration (WPA) allotted projects to the Greer area designed to create jobs to perform necessary work. Local federal work programs included the dredging of waterways for flood control, establishment of a sewing room, and construction of outdoor sanitary toilets on the mill

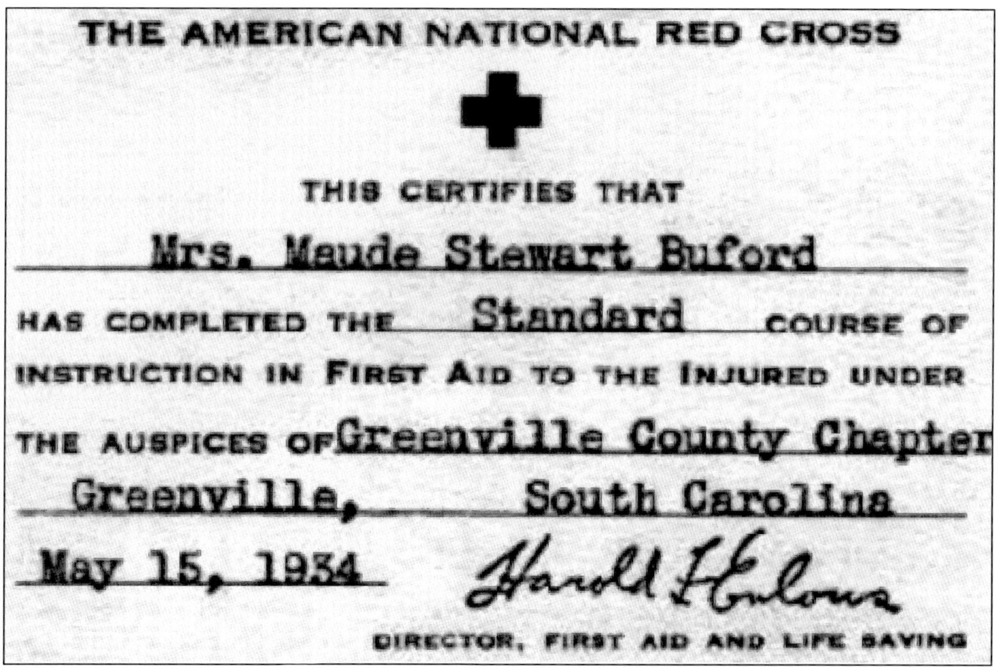

THE AMERICAN NATIONAL RED CROSS

THIS CERTIFIES THAT

Mrs. Maude Stewart Buford

HAS COMPLETED THE Standard COURSE OF INSTRUCTION IN FIRST AID TO THE INJURED UNDER THE AUSPICES OF Greenville County Chapter Greenville, South Carolina

May 15, 1934

Harold F. Enlows

DIRECTOR, FIRST AID AND LIFE SAVING

*THE RED CROSS IN GREER. The Depression that followed the stock market crash required local organizations to dispense aid to suffering families. Greer Relief was organized specifically to meet the needs during hard times; the local chapter of the Red Cross was organized during the First World War.*

villages. The WPA sewing room, under supervision of Anna Riboud, remained in operation until 1940. Located in the hall over C&D Chevrolet Company on Poinsett Street, it was closed ostensibly because South Carolina had a greater quota than average. In reality, the economy had revived considerably. The mayor, council, and chamber of commerce all protested the closing, but to no avail. By that time, the mills were able to take up the slack left by the sewing room.

Other WPA projects included the new post office on South Main Street, the high school stadium, and the new Davenport Memorial Library that opened in September 1938. After the Davenport family gave the land, the community raised private and public funds to erect the first building in Greenville County designed to be a library. Greenville Library used an old school building.

The largest and longest-lived government project in Greer was the Civilian Conservation Corps (CCC) work. Camp Highland, located just north of the town on the Isham Mayfield property, provided labor for farm and forest land reclamation. An announcement that Greer would have a CCC camp located nearby was made in Spartanburg on March 22, 1934. Designed to accommodate 150 men, the camp opened on July 3, 1934. Dr. T.S. Buie, a 1917 Clemson graduate, was named regional director over several camps, including the Greer camp.

A preliminary survey identified the South Tyger River drainage basin as depleted land in need of reclamation. Cotton farmers had over-planted the land for decades. The extensive project ranged from just south of Tigerville to south of Woodruff, encompassing over 120 square miles. The Greer camp served as a base of operations and chief engineer J.T. McAlister planned the day-to-day work. Methods of combating erosion consisted of damming gullies, building terraces, and planting trees.

Life in the camp was much along the lines of a boot camp for military personnel. Young men between the ages of 16 and 25 were selected under a quota system to sign up for a period of manual labor in exchange for bed, board, and a small salary, all but $5 of which was sent home to their families each pay period. Commonly referred to as "soldiers," CCC men took instruction from sergeants and followed a reasonably disciplined work schedule.

Property just off then Ballenger Road north of Greer, leased from Eula Mayfield, was the site of Camp Highland. A road cut into the property looped around the camp located at the loop now known as Princess Circle. Today, the CCC Camp Road is a part of the old Ballenger Road. From 1934 to 1940, this was the perimeter road with barracks, kitchen, and mess hall located inside the loop, and warehouses and non-commissioned officers' quarters located on the outside.

The first men to occupy the camp consisted of Company 441 from Parr Shoals, a camp 20 miles south of Columbia. Among those who arrived in 1934 was First Sergeant John R. Curry Sr. Curry had entered the CCC as a trainee the year before and was sent to the Isle of Palms for further training and immunizations. Once training completed, he was promoted and assigned to Parr Shoals where he served a year.

The term of service for the CCC was six months, in order to give jobs to as many young men as possible. Necessary personnel such as mess and supply sergeants were exempt from the service term as well as supervisors, as needed. Because of the depressed economic conditions, Curry remained with the CCC for seven years. He was in charge of between 40 and 50 of the 200 stationed at Camp Highland. Each day at 7 a.m., men left camp in trucks for work in the field until 5 p.m. A midday meal was served at the work sites. Whether conservation work was performed on public or private lands, there was no cost to landowners.

During free time, men could use the facilities of a small recreation hall located near the edge of the camp where they could read, listen to the radio, and visit with family members on weekends. On Saturday nights, men could attend social events in Greer at their option. Likewise, Sundays were free for worship in area churches. The men occasionally attended public dances in Greer and enjoyed an active baseball competition among area camps. Camp Highland was in a league of upstate CCC camps that included Laurens, Switzer, Abbeville, Greenwood, and Cleveland. In May 1936, Camp Highland had won more that it had lost and was two games behind league-leading Switzer.

The relationship between Greer and Camp Highland was evidently much like that of any town and a nearby military base: elements of isolation from one another with an admixture of welcome and caution. A few CCC men remained in the area; some met their wives in Greer, but for the most part, men returned to their homes after their terms ended. Camp Highland had a turnover rate of about six months because of the service term. By 1935, the state quota for CCC work was a little over 1,000 and the Greer camp had 34 vacancies at the beginning of June.

In 1939, the camp underwent a downward shift in population as conservation projects in the area were completed and work focused on the southern and western parts of the county. That year, Sergeant Curry was sent to a camp at Fountain Inn where he remained a final year before his discharge. Curry later used his CCC skills as director in the physical plant department of Wofford College where he worked for 31 years.

By early 1940, Camp Highland closed and the buildings dismantled for use elsewhere; only the concrete foundations were left. Another New Deal program, the National Youth Administration (NYA), followed the CCC and focused upon providing textile education to boys who qualified. When Parker High School was selected as the site for an NYA center, two Camp Highland barracks, each measuring 120 feet by 30 feet, were reassembled at the Parker High campus. Many of the young men of the CCC enlisted or were drafted into military service as the Depression ended and threat of war appeared.

The effects of the Depression also began to be felt locally in the schools. While Greer School District seemed to be in command of its destiny, the priorities of its building program and its conservative fiscal policies during the previous decade had left no reserves for the Great Depression. The year 1931 was significant for Greer education because the second installment of state aid under the 6-0-1 plan occurred. Of 88 districts in the county, Greer received the third highest amount,

$6,282, after Greenville and Parker Districts. The much-needed funds came at a time when local schools were running behind in their obligations. Greer was only $40.24 in arrears. The 6-0-1 Law was a fiscal boost to the local district, but it required Greer to enroll 130 pupils from outside the district, but adjacent and conveniently located to Greer schools. Despite the 6-0-1 plan, Greer was unable to find additional needed funds during the 1931–1932 term, and the schools were scheduled to close for lack of funds on April 1, 1932. The Farmers and Taxpayers League protested. W.P. Conyers, president, suggested notes or vouchers-script, anything short of repudiation of contracts, which would damage the system as well as the credit of the state.

Greer did not close the doors of its schools, but teachers went unpaid for a time and the district did limit the number of contracts issued for the next academic year for only the months the money could cover. With fewer teachers, conditions for learning worsened, but the system in Greer remained intact. As the impact of the failing economy hit closer to home, local teachers' pay was cut 12.5 percent across the board for the 1932–1933 session. Superintendent S.W. Rabb announced the opening of schools would be on September 7 because of the crowded conditions and fewer teachers. Only those residing in the Greer District would be permitted to enroll in a Greer school and no exceptions were made. Rabb hoped, but made no promises, for a nine-month term. In 1934, Superintendent Rabb reported Greer City School pupil population at 1,302. Without additional monies, the district could not operate a full term. An act of the legislature approved on March 19, 1934 permitted Greer trustees to levy a district tax of up to 22 mils, an increase of only three mils above what Greer had previously levied.

B.H. McFadden of Spartanburg served as the principal of Greer's school for African-American children. Arriving in Greer in 1930, McFadden and former principal Sullivan proposed to the school board that the school be named in honor of poet Paul Lawrence Dunbar. The years of hardship were difficult for black education in Greer. With little funding for construction and maintenance, the building fell into disrepair. White school population decreased by about 25 percent while the population of black school-age children increased.

By 1936, the Dunbar School consisted of 9 teachers and over 300 pupils. Trustees of Greer School District approved a motion on September 10, 1936, authorizing a two-teacher school for the Needmore community if patrons could provide the building. Ms. Theopia Goodlett and Minnie J. Griffin of the Dunbar faculty were selected as teachers, and B.D. Henson provided a building lot. Residents of the Needmore Community raised the funds, secured the land, and gave it to the board cost-free. Community leaders petitioned the board to construct a small school on the lot as soon as possible, but funds for contraction were not immediately available, delaying construction indefinitely.

At Dunbar, Principal B.H. McFadden remained until the 1940 term. His replacement was William Bankhead, who came from Taylor's school. During his last year, McFadden had supervised seven teachers during the eight-month school term. State funding provided for the first seven months; the local district paid for an additional month. Local supplements for white teachers ranged between $180 and $405, while local supplement for blacks was pegged at $50 per teacher. The lowest paid white administrator received $2,100 compared to McFadden's $600. In 1939, the 11th grade was added at Dunbar, giving African-American students in the district roughly equivalent educational opportunity in terms of length of schooling.

All schools in the district deteriorated during the war years. In a June 1941 letter from his army post, Superintendent William M. Albergotti recommended replacement of the porches at the "Colored School" that had been patched and repatched over the years. In the same letter, he noted that the white high school toilets, a perennial problem, had been unchanged since the building of the school in 1922 and were in need of attention.

Again in spring 1941, the board considered building a small school for the children of the Needmore community. At an April meeting, Secretary B.B. Waters raised the matter and, in June, the board asked the chairman to get a plan for a small school. Lack of interest, the scarcity of funds, and the approaching war were factors in the board's decisions to repair existing structures rather than build new ones. The final prewar improvement to Dunbar was approval of a shelving project.

*PAPER DRIVE: DAVENPORT HIGH. The Second World War required united efforts of everyone, at home and on the battlefront. During America's earliest experience with recycling, Greer High students collected paper for re-processing as shown here about 1943.*

By the eve of war, all classes and both races had shared years of hardship. The relief effort of the early 1930s had become both generalized and democratized. In December 1939, Parks Boozer, scoutmaster of troop 39, and his boy scouts collected toys, and R.P. Turner's wholesale grocery business furnished candy for needy children. Nor was the town's generosity restricted to children. Civic clubs, social circles, scout troops, and others collected and distributed food, fuel, and clothing to 274 people through Greer Relief. Greer Relief presented a Christmas tree to the WPA sewing room ladies.

By this time, Greer Relief extended aid and comfort to the African-American communities and worked with their leaders, such as Blanche Thompson. With the help of other volunteers, Thompson rigged a truck with a lighted Christmas tree, placed a small organ on the truck, and drove to the homes of the elderly to sing Christmas carols and distribute candy and fruit. Turner's company again supplied the candy and the Young Men's Bible Class of the First Baptist Church supplied the fruit. The truck and carolers left the home of the Greer Relief secretary Mrs. J.G. Buford at 5 a.m. Christmas morning to visit 60 homes.

By 1940, Greer had achieved maturity as a small town. It had undergone successive re-definitions after its humble origin as a crossroads community. From a collection of general stores to a viable town with a country cotton market and then a mill town, Greer represented progress and achievement. Weathering the Depression even as its major industry came near collapse, Greer was on the brink of economic recovery and prosperity.

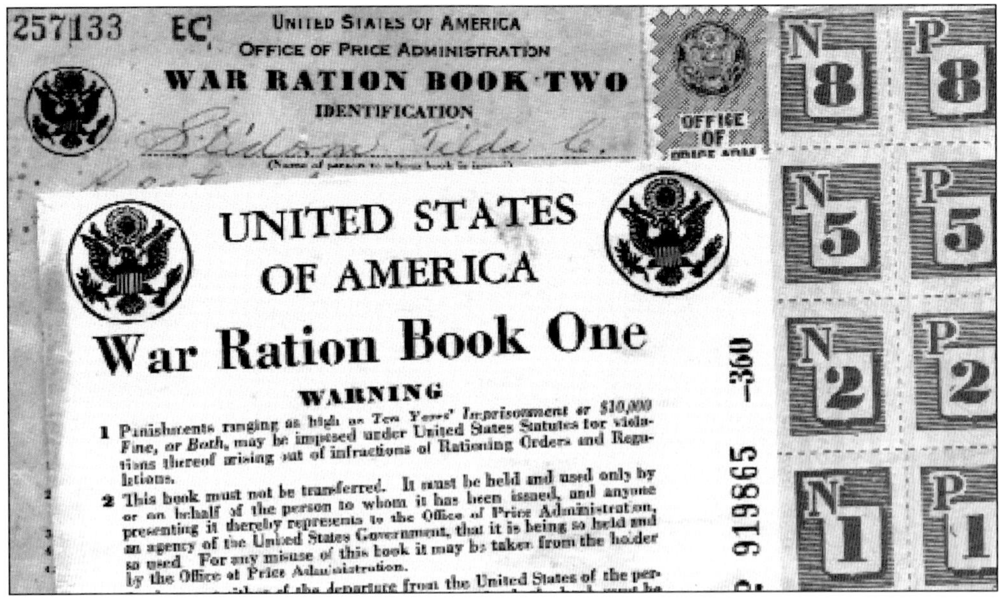


*WAR RATION STAMPS. To assure the war effort, gasoline, tires, and foodstuffs were rationed during the war. To make purchases, stamps such as those pictured were required with the price of the item.*

While the war required the services and even the lives of many area men, it lifted the country from the Depression and gave opportunity to segments of society that, for generations, had little expectation of prosperity. Victor-Monaghan mills became defense plants, as did McCall Manufacturing, on the site of the old Franklin Mill. Greer, like other towns across the country, prepared for civil defense. Cotton mill operatives worked overtime as necessary to manufacture bandage, uniform, canvas, and utility materials for the war effort. Labor was long and intense; food and consumer goods were sharply rationed.

World War II disrupted Greer to a far greater extent than the previous war. Men, who were called to duty by law or conscience, left behind jobs and families, in some cases never to return. The scope of the war and the transient nature of the population make any complete historical account of all specific contributions of Greer area combat soldiers difficult. Greer area men served in all branches and were represented in all tallies: killed, wounded, missing in action, and prisoners of war. Returning soldiers brought with them scars, wounds (some fatal even years later), medals, memories, and even wives.

Among those who did not return from service were Carroll E. Belcher and James Wilkerson, Greer's first casualties of World War II. Lieutenant George A. Hamrick was killed in action in October 1943. Joseph O. Campbell died in France on December 23, 1944; Raymond Cannon died at the Battle of Iwo Jima. Surgeon Allen Bennett, son of banker B.A. Bennett, was killed in action at Ormoc Bay off Leyte Gulf. Others who died while in service include Paul Jones Adams, gunner mate third class of Pelham; Arthur J. Alexander, United States Marine Corps Reserve; James H. Crouse; Lee Roy Cox; Harmon M. Gilstrap; and Nelson F. Heiligert. Other known individuals from Greer who served during World War II are listed in the appendix.

When war loomed large in America's prospects, the country instituted a peacetime draft to bolster its defenses. Local draft board 39 was headed by E.C. Bailey and met in the hall over C&D Chevrolet. On May 20, 1941, in executive order No. 8757, Roosevelt created the Office of Civilian Defense. Across the state, local councils were established at the city and county levels. The Spartanburg County Council included Greer Mayor H.J. Lanford, while R.B. Dean was the Greer member of the Greenville County Council.

The Home Guard, as local councils were collectively called, was based in part on a similar British organization. Greer formed a council of civilian defense with Dr. Johnny Walker, proprietor of the Greer Drug Company, serving as chairman. B.M. Lanford was commander of the Citizens Defense Corps, and Mrs. J.G. Buford was executive director of the Citizens Service Corps. The Civil Defense trained and posted air raid wardens, and planned for emergency auxiliary police and fire protection.

Every aspect of life was altered for the duration of the European crisis and possible war, including the operation of the schools. Superintendent Albergotti was captain in National Guard Battery A, 178th Field Artillery at Greer when called to active duty in January 1941. The school board gave him an indefinite

*ENSIGN CARROLL BELCHER. A naval navigator stationed at Pearl Harbor, Belcher was killed when his plane was lost during a mission on July 16, 1942.*

leave of absence. While his duties permitted, he continued to direct school affairs from his military station. Shortly after Albergotti was called to service, the board selected as interim superintendent the principal of Davenport High School, R.L. Stuart. A native of Coronaca, Stuart had to administer the school budget of almost $8 million. J.G. Hayes, principal of Central Elementary, replaced Stuart at the high school. Students at Davenport High School were also quick to answer the call of their country and a number of the 1942 graduating class enlisted prior to graduation for immediate transport to training camp after receiving their diplomas.

Other district employees who left to answer the call of the nation included Wister Smith, Orvil Duncan, and Julius Hodges, whose resignations were taken as of June 12, 1942. At least one female teacher left to marry her fiancé before he shipped out. Chairman Taylor of the school board wrote E.C. Bailey, chairman of Selective Service Board 39 of Greer, in November, asking for a deferment for David Sheppard, the band director, who had received his draft notice. Band directors were in especially short supply. Taylor made it clear that Sheppard did not know of the request, but less than two weeks later, the Japanese attacked Pearl Harbor, rendering the request moot. No exceptions were made.

By the time Pearl Harbor was bombed, many Greer men were already serving in an active duty national guard or had joined the regular service. The ominous threat of Adolph Hitler prompted better behavior among the public for a reduction in crime at all levels. Alcohol did not go away, but during wartime, there was more "drinking for a reason," as one individual explained it. Some magistrates, particularly at the beginning of the war, gave minor miscreants the option of serving their time on the chain gang or in the military. By the time of Chief Tapp's resignation on April 13, 1942, Greer was as sober and orderly as it had ever been.

Greer citizens reacted to the attack on Pearl Harbor by increasing their level of readiness to meet any threat. On February 10, the council gave the mayor emergency powers to call out National Civilian Defense Forces if necessary. The city council donated $100 in cash to the home guard and voted to supply them

*PRINCIPAL R.L. STUART. R.L. Stuart, who served as an athletic coach and administrator, filled in for Superintendent Albergotti during the Second World War.*

with 20 pairs of shoes. Greer Civilian Defense Organization was reorganized and approved on May 12, 1942 under leadership of Mayor Fred Crow. J.S. Paget, controller, coordinated work with the mill villages and B.M. Lanford was chief air raid warden. Other divisions were established to create an auxiliary police and fire department, utilities, medical necessities, and finance sections.

Unit leaders attended special training classes to prepare for possible attack on American soil. John A. Robinson was the senior gas officer in Greer whose duties included detecting an attack using gas warfare, protecting the citizenry from gas, and organizing evacuation. Milledge Brannon, Charlie Kendrick, Roy C. Taylor, and R.B. Wood were bomb reconnaissance agents; their responsibilities were to locate and identify unexploded aerial bombs and evacuate endangered citizens. Coastal evacuees would come to three designated areas. Greer was in Reception Area B and would provide temporary housing. In keeping with the custom of the times, evacuees were to be assigned to houses according to race.

From the declaration of war until its end, local citizens passed not a day without thinking of the events overseas. The Civilian Defense Council organized frequent air raid warnings and practice blackouts, coordinating these with cotton mills, which were permitted to remain lighted unless certain signals indicated the real thing. Newspapers were filled with little else; the radio, the popular media, and the entertainment business continued, but with orientation toward winning the war. Advertisements took on patriotic colors.

The Service Corps issued ration cards, planted victory gardens, and organized scrap metal collection and a "share your car" campaign. On January 1, 1942, the Office of Production Management froze all new car and truck sales. While the mills increased hours and payrolls swelled, so did the number of items on the ration list. Reminiscent of World War I was concern for security even at the local level in small towns. The cotton mills of Greer became defense plants as uniform and bandage material flowed from their looms. Employees were required to wear photo identification badges when reporting to work and to cooperate with gate men. Censors often mutilated letters arriving from loved ones in service if information therein was considered sensitive. Phone communication was precious between family and servicemen. Public phones available at the bus depot at the Wayside Hotel provided a means for servicemen and loved ones to speak on the eve of the soldier's departure for the war. Through letters, families would set a time when they would be at the hotel to receive a call from sons, husbands, and brothers. Families without phones often swamped the hotel on weekends.

On August 27, 1942, a serviceman's center was set up in the basement of the Davenport Memorial Library on School Street. The large room had ping pong and card tables, a piano, and a 5¢ jukebox. Over the fireplace hung the flags of the Allies. The center was open Saturday nights and all day Sunday.

During the war years, school curriculum prepared students to live in a world torn by war. All male students anticipated military service by their 18th birthday whether graduated or not. Beginning with the 1942–1943 term, training in pre-flight aeronautics was added to the curriculum.

*USO CLUB. The basement of the Davenport Memorial Library was converted from a meeting room to a United Service Organization hall for the benefit of servicemen passing through Greer during the Second World War. A hostess poses with several soldiers in the library's backyard.*

August Avery "Gus" Finley was Greer's wartime chief of police. A Pickens native, Finley was a World War I veteran and 20-year officer, who had become the day officer in 1939 when the highly regarded Charlie Liverett retired because of health. By 1941, Finley was promoted to assistant chief and sworn in as chief on May 1, 1942. A large and easygoing man, Finley had a reputation as a "man of his word" and a "no-nonsense" officer. Known among other officers as "two-gun Gus," he carried a backup revolver at a time when many officers complained about the weight of the heavy revolvers they normally wore as a sidearm. His tenure included the war years when travel was heavy through the depots of Greer. During the war years, law enforcement focused upon cafes or "joints," hotels, and pool halls, all of which attracted bootleggers and prostitutes. Greer remained relatively orderly during wartime, and despite preparations made by the Home Guard, it was never necessary to call in auxiliary police officers. Still, some volunteers "shadowed" Chief Finley and other officers to learn the routine of police work.

The spirit of patriotism ran high in Greer during the war. Air Force week was celebrated in Greer from April 5 to April 10, 1943, with speeches, meals, and music to honor veterans and men about to go to war. The week began with a War Bond rally on Monday at the intersection of Trade and Poinsett Streets.

SOLDIER IN RHINELAND. *Seargent Thomas McAbee sits on a curb in the Rhineland, spring 1945. McAbee, 4th Infantry Division, saw action in five European campaigns 1943–1945, earned sergeants' stripes, the Purple Heart with Oak Leaf Cluster, and the Bronze Star.*

The streets were blocked, a dais constructed in front of B.A. Bennett Insurance Company where Governor Olin Johnston addressed the crowd of perhaps 2,000 who filled the streets, hung out of second-story windows, and even sat on the roofs of nearby buildings. The band from Camp Croft provided military and patriotic music for the occasion. The Grand Theater, which was showing the movie *Air Force* starring John Garfield, had its marquee proclaim that "every American should see it."

After the Normandy invasion, the Civilian Defense Councils were abolished. At war's end, celebration in Greer was muted, compared with that after World War I. Greer's Civilian Defense Council was disbanded and its residual funds were donated in 1950 to Greer High School to be used in the purchase of band uniforms. The Servicemen's Center continued to operate at the library until January 1946. When it closed, it had provided entertainment for over 6,000 servicemen. On Christmas Day, 1945, 20 or more soldiers stranded in Greer from states as distant as Texas and New York were given free phone privileges for calls to family, courtesy of the citizens of Greer.

At war's end, the school board reelected Superintendent Albergotti to head the Greer School District. Since he was not yet mustered out, it became necessary to hire J.H. Koon as temporary principal of the grammar school for the fall 1945 term. During his term of service, Albergotti had risen in rank to colonel, seen service in southern Europe, and earned medals for bravery. When the board prepared to return Stuart and Hayes to their former positions, Albergotti declined to return, choosing instead to remain in the army. This decision, he noted, was difficult after having served the district for more than 16 years.

For the merchants and industrial workers of Greer, the wartime economy brought greater prosperity. Years of rationing and deprivation, filled with much overtime work, permitted savings to accumulate. Wartime prosperity compensated for years of depression and gave the mill worker the ability to own his own home, thus helping to expand the middle class during the postwar years.

*MARINE AT CAMP PENDLETON. Marine Private David L. Belcher shipped out from Camp Pendleton and served 25 months in the Pacific theater as a field radio operator. He returned a lance corporal.*

# 8. Recovery, Diversification, and Growth: 1946–Present

From the end of World War II through the 1960s, Greer was a lively business center largely propelled by the payrolls of surrounding textile communities. The accumulated savings of servicemen and civilian workers contributed to a new wave of expansion for Greer, largely in residential building. For the most part, Greer had never experienced fundamental change in its economy or social structure. Over the decades, it remained dependent upon a form of the cotton trade. Subtly, as technology intervened, the population had become dependent upon the factory rather than the farm. The production of textile products was still the basis for life in Greer. During the two decades after World War II, a generation grew to maturity and entered the local workforce, expecting life to continue for them as it had for their parents and grandparents. That expectation did not materialize nor did Greer retain its provincial character.

At the end of fiscal year 1946, the assets of the Bank of Greer rose to over $6 million. Despite bank failures of the previous decade, customers flocked to do business at a financial institution they perceived as being both conservative and adaptive. As the cotton trade diminished in importance, full-time farming virtually ceased except for larger landholders. The bank concentrated upon marketing its services to small businesses, consumers, and automobile buyers and offered competitive rates of interest to savings account holders. Savings accounts became very popular with the generation that had weathered the Depression.

Business in Greer continued to be conducted on Saturdays. Men from the mill villages and farmers squatted and sat on the ledges around the Bank of Greer awaiting George Gibbs, the African-American janitor, to open the doors. On a typical Saturday, farmers and mill hands gathered at the bank to discuss world affairs, while women and children shopped until lunch. Families had several options for meals, ranging from Tony Taleff's Sanitary Cafe just north of the P&N tracks, to the Elite on the 200 block of Trade, or Creight Taylors' (later Lewis' Drive-In). Food was also available at the Wayside Inn and later at the Dixie Lunch and the Coffee Pot Restaurant. "Meat and three" (vegetables) with refills of iced sweet tea ran in the neighborhood of 75¢. Before the era of the day

*WAYSIDE INN. Built during the Depression, the Wayside Inn saw heavy use by military personnel during the Second World War. It continued to serve after the war as well.*

care facility, the movies served to confine and monitor children during Saturday afternoon when the playbill included favorites such as a Roy Rogers western and Ma and Pa Kettle comedies. Managers Reginald Chesson and Bill Drace of the Greer and Grande Theaters, respectively, maintained order and offered soft drinks and a box of popcorn for 15¢. African-American patrons were welcome to sit in the balcony at each theater. Often, a family completed the day in Greer with a visit to Ponder's Ice Cream Parlor for a "cream" or a cup of orange ice.

After the war, a novel form of entertainment, the drive-in theater, became popular in Greer. Two drive-ins were built in Greer, one on each end of town on the newly rerouted national highway, called the "Super Highway" because it had divided four lanes. The Greer Drive-In sat on the former Holtzclaw property where Ryan's corporate offices are now located; the King Cotton was located just east of the Apalache Road intersection.

Regular theaters remained popular during the days when television was still out of reach of most people, and the drive-in had neither heating nor air conditioning. The Greer Theater opened in 1949 under the management of Earl Russell. An Everett Enterprises theater, it became a part of the Stewart and Everett chain, operating for two decades before television and multi-screen theaters in larger cities rendered it obsolete. Both the Greer and the Grand Theaters operated on a two-day schedule, showing four movies a week with a double feature plus cartoon and short subject (newsreel) being shown on Friday and Saturday. The theaters, like most other Greer businesses—except drugstores—were closed Sundays. A few drive-in restaurants on the Super Highway opened after church hours. In 1949, Greer refined its cultural identity further when a local radio station, WEAB, an enterprise of E.A. Burch, owner of the *Greer Citizen*, went on air in mid-year.

# LEWIS' DRIVE-IN

| SANDWICHES | | SHORT ORDERS (Include French Fries and Slaw) | |
|---|---|---|---|
| Sliced Barbecue | 50c | | |
| Minced Barbecue | 45c | Oyster Fry | 1.40c |
| Roast Pork | 50c | Steak/Country Style | 1.10c |
| Hamburger | 40c | Steak | 1.10c |
| Hamburger/N. O. | 40c | Hamburger Steak | 1.10c |
| Hamburg/Let. Tom. | 40c | ½ Fry Chicken | 1.55c |
| Cheeseburger | 45c | ¼ Fry Chicken | 1.10c |
| Cheesebur/Let. Tom. | 45c | Chicken Livers | 1.25 |
| Hot Dogs | 25c | Shrimp | 1.40c |
| Hot Dog/N. O. | 25c | Fish "Perch" | 1.10c |
| Bacon, Let., Tom. | 45c | | |
| Lettuce and Tomato | 30c | Ham and Eggs | 85c |
| Cheese/Pimiento | 35c | Bacon and Eggs | 85c |
| Steak/Country Style | 50c | Hot Roast Pork | 1.00 |
| Ham | 50c | Barbecue Hash | 1.00 |
| Potato Chips | 10c | **DRINKS** | |
| Chicken San. | 50c | Coca-Cola | 15c |
| French Fries P/O | 30c | Dr. Pepper | 15c |
| Egg | 30c | Seven-Up | 15c |
| Fish | 50c | Grape | 15c |
| Ham and Egg | 55c | Pepsi-Cola | 15c |
| Bacon and Egg | 50c | Orange | 15c |
| Chili Sandwich | 20c | Milk | 15c |
| Steak/Cover Wagon | 50c | Chocolate Milk | 15c |
| Soups | 35c | | |
| Jumbo Hamburger | 65c | Coffee | 15c |
| Jumbo Cheeseburger | 70c | Tomato Juice | 15c |
| **ICE CREAM** | | Orange Juice | 15c |
| Chocolate | 15c | | |
| Vanilla | 15c | Iced Tea | 15c |
| Strawberry | 15c | **MALTS** | |
| Cherry | 15c | Chocolate | 35c |
| Butter Pecan | 15c | Vanilla | 35c |
| | | Strawberry | 35c |
| Banana Split | 50c | Cherry | 35c |
| Nut Sundae | 35c | Pineapple | 35c |
| Ice 5c & | 10c | Pie | |
| **CIGARETTES** | | **CHEWING GUM** | |

*LEWIS' MENU. Before the "McDonaldization" of Greer, there were a number of local cafes and restaurants offering substantial fare at modest prices. Tony Tallef's Sanitary Restaurant served the finest hot dogs on earth at his counter while Lewis Gosnell offered a wide variety of selections at his Drive-In, as shown by this order pad from the 1960s.*

Greer began to experience significant change almost immediately after the war. In 1946, the Greer School District, following the loss of a longtime superintendent, lost accreditation for the high school when Davenport High School lost its membership in the Southern Association of Schools and Colleges, after having been a member school since 1925. Reasons cited were insufficient library training, overcrowded classrooms (some with 40 or more pupils), and unqualified teachers in the classroom. Already warned years earlier of the possibility of having accreditation pulled because of over-crowding, Greer School District was operating poorly at the limit of its resources. Superintendent Stuart requested use of the Davenport Memorial Library basement for one year to relieve crowding at Central Elementary.

No rent was charged, but the district agreed to renovate the room as a condition for its use. Although the district never did complete its contract to renovate, it was permitted to use the building for four years.

Although Greer schools regained accreditation in 1947, Greer residents realized that some action had to be taken to assure that the district did not suffer this problem again. Financially, the local district was still not sound. After the war, a federal program to enable veterans to return to night school to obtain their diplomas brought in needed funds. The two-year influx of federal money allowed the board to balance its budget in 1948. A 1949 bond issue of $125,000 was approved for the construction of new high schools for blacks and whites. New trends were growing signs of change in race relations. At Christmas time, 1947, when public officials were given bonuses, both black and white teachers received $10 from the Greer District, a nod to the concept of equality under law, although the local school district prepared to continue to administer its schools on a "separate but equal basis."

There was some hope that the district would receive a windfall from the fortune of William W. Burgess, Greer cotton mill magnate and second millionaire who had died in 1945. Burgess had envisioned either a school or hospital resting on the hillside where his peach orchard had been, a place he had named Air Castle Heights in memory of his son. Instead, a 1949 court decision permitted the sale of the land for development as Greer's premier upscale residential community, known today as Burgess Hills.

*VICTOR ELEMENTARY, KATE WILSON'S CLASS. The mill schools remained in operation until population shifts required new schools be built nearer Highway 29, the principal thoroughfare after 1960. Shown is Kate Wilson's class at Victor Elementary School, 1955.*

Questions arose about the ability of the district to continue to meet local educational needs. The strength of consolidated districts had been promoted since early in the century in various parts of the South. The issue was argued anew during the late 1940s as the 80-odd districts of the county struggled to supply their schools with needed equipment and materials. In 1949, the County Legislative Delegation, which served in the capacity of a county council, appointed a 15-person committee to study the administration of schools within the county. At the time, there were 86 districts. Two of the districts, Greenville City and Parker District, served two-thirds of the county's children. Greer Superintendent Charles H. Chewning, who succeeded R.L. Stuart, served on the committee, which also included L.P. Hollis. In June 1950, the committee endorsed the consolidation, but called for a gradual approach to something less than total consolidation

Nearby rural schools were in similar straits. North of Greer, Jordan High School was reported in 1949 to be suffering from physical decay, needed repairs, crowding, and lack of equipment. Moreover, small districts possessed a range of physical quality and financial ability that made for inequities in the educational product within the county. Yet, just as important was the democratic tradition that permitted communities to establish schools and maintain local control of them. Double Springs, Ansel, Jordan, Washington, and others held fast to the right to determine not only what was taught, but also who taught it. In rural communities, the school was the center where the children learned and the community met, danced, and voted.

The first action on consolidation of schools took place in Greer area districts. "Youthful administrators" Charles Chewning and B.L. Frick oversaw the first consolidation in the county, which became official July 1, 1950 as six rural districts joined with Greer. Victor, Apalache, Zoar, Pelham, Ansel, and Pleasant Grove added over 1,000 children and 100 teachers to the Greer District. Chewning of Bishopville had left the principal position at Fountain Inn to come to Greer. Frick, former superintendent-principal of Ninety-Six schools, came to Greer initially as principal of Davenport High School.

The majority of the county's citizens initially opposed the consolidation with a vote held on July 11, 1950. Despite the public's voice, the General Assembly passed a General School Law, Act 379, in early 1951, which gave the County Board of Education the authority to consolidate the small districts of the county. The consolidation was completed on August 23, 1951. Fred Crow was the Greer representative on the county board.

Public reaction varied. In Jordan community, the people "were not very enthusiastic about it." In Greer, people initially did not like the idea, but there were no fights, nor lingering hatred. One reason may have been that consolidation was done on paper, but only actual construction would bring it into reality. Where possible, elements of local influence were retained. Community leaders of the 80-odd districts of the county were persuaded that only through consolidation would modern school buildings be made available to the students of the county.

*PRINCIPAL B.L. FRICK, 1950. B.L. Frick came to Greer initially as principal of Davenport High School and later Greer Senior High. In his many years as administrator, his favorite descriptor of academic and extra-curricular events was always the same: "mighty-fine." His thousands of former wards consider him to have been a "mighty-fine" principal.*

The board appointed area superintendents to assure citizens that the basic elements of continuity would not disappear into a larger bureaucracy.

Blue Ridge and Greer High Schools were built; Blue Ridge to handle consolidation of country schools in the northeastern county, Greer Senior High to handle growth of greater Greer. Consolidation brought loss of tradition for some students and loss of employment for some educators, at least temporarily. In 1954, Jordan closed and students transferred to Blue Ridge. Principal Lewis Phillips, receiving no contract at the new school, had to wait until 1956 when he came to Greer High as teacher and athletic coach.

School consolidation did not alleviate all the problems associated with localism. Students at Reid School, halfway between Greenville and Greer, continued to use outdoor toilets for another four years after consolidation. Nor were all the inequities between black and white schools addressed. Within three years, consolidation did, however, make possible the construction of Lincoln High School, a new school for African-American students of the Greer area.

By the 1950s, the public nationally began to question the Jim Crow system that had been given birth by the Supreme Court in 1896. Commemorative coinage honored Booker T. Washington and George Washington Carver. The Democratic Party, under the leadership of J. Strom Thurmond, split over the method of dealing with the race issue. In 1954, the Supreme Court invalidated the

*GREER HIGH 1952. The new high school was dedicated March 8, 1953.*

legal bases for Jim Crow laws, but the national trends had little immediate impact upon Greer. Few African Americans held industrial jobs and those who worked for the city held lower-level positions. At Christmas time during the early 1950s, when bonuses were awarded to city employees, blacks received $7.50 to white employees' $10. Under the leadership of Lloyd Hunt, a public housing project began in 1951 to improve the condition of the poorer neighborhoods.

Besides public housing, one of the most significant building programs of the 1950s that improved life in Greer was the building of Allen Bennett Hospital. After the closing of Chick Springs Hospital, Greer remained without a hospital for two decades. During the interim, patients were seen by doctors, who regularly made house calls, or in critical cases, were transported either to Greenville or Spartanburg hospitals by ambulance. Construction on a $500,000, 27-bed hospital was begun in December 1950. On May 1, 1952, Allen Bennett Hospital opened its doors to receive new patients. Built on land donated by Belton A. Bennett, the facility was named for his son, who was killed during World War II. During the next four decades, the hospital was enlarged three times, adding 110 beds. The hospital facility enabled Greer to attract additional resident medical personnel.

Law enforcement, as well as public health, had always been a challenge in Greer from earliest days because of its location astride a county line. Greer City Council had requested and received assistance from the highway patrol as well as from deputies of both Greenville and Spartanburg Counties in the past. Officers who filled newly created positions and vacant ones left by retiring officers were often military veterans of the recent war. Henry Sammons, Howell Davis, David Belcher, John D. Black, T. Greene Howard, Alton Howard, and others filled the ranks in the late 1940s and early 1950s. These new young officers brought a degree of responsibility and discipline that meshed well with the maturity and experience of officers such as Chief Gus Finely and Lieutenant Vernon Davis. The result was that the overall effectiveness of the department improved and citizens held it in high regard.

Safety was given high priority during Gus Finley's seven-year tenure as chief. A chamber of commerce safety committee partnered with the police department for a traffic safety program for children. Student safety patrols were active at both black and white elementary schools from the late 1940s to 1956. After Chief Finley's health failed in early 1949 and he died in August, Roy L. Lister was sworn in on August 31, 1949. Lister, a former Spartanburg County magistrate, had served as a Spartanburg County deputy since 1937 before coming to work at Greer in April 1947 as a lieutenant under Chief Finley. Lister was the first college man to serve in the Greer department, having attended the University of South Carolina.

The textile mills located near Greer all came under new management shortly after the end of World War II. One of the first moves made by the new owner, J.P. Stevens Company, was to offer the mill village houses for sale at each of the

*BOOTLEG HAUL. Officers Henry Sammens (kneeling) and Alton Howard (standing) examine a car trunk full of bootleg whiskey seized by Greer officers during a 1953 traffic check.*

former Victor-Monaghan Mills near Greer. The prices of 40- or 50-year-old mill cottages were reasonable enough that many mill operatives became homeowners, adding dimensions of pride and creating a degree of social pressure on the merchant class. This transfer of property also made it possible for the city of Greer to annex contiguous areas into the city limits, increasing its tax base to provide needed municipal services neglected during the Depression and wartime. Greer extended its city limits in 1950 and 1951, increasing its area from .80 to 2.45 square miles, which tripled the area and doubled the population of Greer. One of the first needed improvements to the infrastructure was a $1-million expansion of utilities overseen by Public Works superintendent Carl Landford. A larger town also required more services, including police and fire protection and street maintenance. While Greer continued to rely largely upon a volunteer fire department and small street crew, the city did purchase a new fire truck and sanitation vehicle to improve services for local citizens.

During the 1950s, juvenile crime was a primary concern, mostly in petty thefts and driving violations, primarily speeding on city streets. The Lions, Kiwanis, and Exchange Clubs of Greer donated a safety car to the department on June 23, 1950. Annexation of new areas into the city both challenged and aided law enforcement. To meet the challenge, the city bought a three-way-radio system in mid-1950, alleviating the need for officers to use a telephone or come back to the station to make reports to the desk officer or a superior. Annexation of the mill villages into the city limits simplified law enforcement by extending city officers' jurisdiction. The police force became necessarily more mobile, and the two cars stayed on the streets virtually 24 hours a day except for changing of the shifts which occurred at 7 a.m., 3 p.m., and 11 p.m. each day. New cars were purchased more often. The city bought a new Ford and a new Pontiac in January 1951. In an effort to meet a tight budget, a Harley-Davidson motorcyle was added in 1953. The personal equipment of each officer included a .38 caliber revolver, one set of cuffs, a wrist chain, and a slapjack.

Despite change during the 1950s, Greer continued much as it had the previous half-century. It was not easy to discern the fading days of agriculture when a few cotton wagons continued to roll into town, making their way to the cotton oil mill south of the railroad tracks. Nor were the emerging class distinctions within the white community obvious as merchants, professionals, and cotton mill executives bought lots and homes in the more exclusive residential developments. Within the textile industry, change had arrived also. Cotton's importance had waned in the wake of new synthetic fibers. The mills in the area could not claim the exclusive title of "cotton mill" any longer, but they kept running, continuing to fuel the economy of a busy downtown Greer. In the 1960s and earlier, many students continued to drop out of school when they reached working age. Local textile mills held promise to third- and fourth-generation operatives; however, as textiles came under assault from foreign competition, jobs were phased out in favor of advancing technology. Proportionately, the level of education required for the operation of

*COMMISSIONERS OF PUBLIC WORKS. The Greer Commission of Public Works, organized in 1914, was supervised by a board of commissioners. Shown are past and present members of the board in this early 1950s photo. From left to right are as follows: (front row) Harry Cunningham, John A. Robinson, Murray Hughes, and J.S. "Sud" Paget; (back row) T. Gordon Smith, Wyatt Fowler, Marion Lanford, Dan Davenport, Carl Lanford (manager).*

complex industrial machinery increased and mills could be more selective in their employment.

College or university was an alternative for relatively few students who followed in their parents' footsteps as merchants, farmers, or mill hands. With the consolidation of schools, the percentage of Greer graduates going on to college dropped considerably as the social class distribution was altered. Practically any education beyond high school was out of the question for the vast majority until the technical centers were introduced during the decade of the 1960s. These institutions gave children of the county and mill villages their first real alternative to following their parents' professions. Already, new industries had arrived in Greer, paying better wages than the mills in some cases. Homelite and Bowers Battery Company also offered a variation on industrial work, which appealed to those who tired easily of breathing textile lint. For a time in the decade of the 1960s, the remnants of farming coexisted with cotton textiles and new industry. The economic strength of Greer had never been stronger.

*GREER POLICE DEPARTMENT, 1954. From left are: (kneeling) Captain Parks Boozer, Lieutenant McCoy Bright, Officers Howell Davis, Fred Anders, Henry Sammons, S.A. Wall, and Bill White; (standing) Officers Wilton Green, David Belcher, Jimmy Hindman, Louie Henderson, Cleo Center, Lieutenant Vernon Davis, Chief Roy Lister, Fire Chief R.B. Colvin, Officer Bill Reid, Lieutenant B.A. Fincher, Officer Alton Howard.*

By the end of 1960s, only one segment, one community, remained to be incorporated into the main stream of larger society and economy—the African-American citizens. Before that could happen, the matter of racial segregation had to be addressed and it made sense that the forefront of racial reform would be the school system whose principal objective was instructing people on how to live with one another.

When the process of desegregation began in 1963, Lincoln High School, as well as other black schools, began to lose identity with the Supreme Court's ruling. When the court order was issued to begin integration, which Judge Robert J. Martin did upon examination of Greenville County School plan, former Greer mayor and member of the county delegation Lloyd Hunt initiated House proceedings to repeal compulsory attendance laws, a merely symbolic effort.

Integration of the schools in Greer proceeded with considerable tension, but without violence. When Dunbar Elementary opened as East Greer Elementary School, white parents converged on Dunbar to scrub and mop it before children were scheduled to attend. It was a largely symbolic gesture motivated as much by resentment as by actual need. Although expected, violence within the local schools did not materialize, although tension remained high. Tensions erupted in an act of arson on February 1970 when Davenport Junior High was burned. Fires, set in three or four areas, gutted the building by early morning.

Twenty-seven Greer firemen and a company from Greenville fought the fire for 14 hours. Volunteers moved much of the equipment from the building even as the fire continued to burn. Gossip blamed the Klan; another theory held African Americans responsible. Ed Burch, editor of *The Greer Citizen*, summarized the local collective feeling: "It is hoped that the person or persons responsible for the fire can be quickly apprehended and brought to justice, whether they be white or black." The 600 students were bussed to Sevier Middle in Taylors to complete the term. In September 1970, Lincoln High School closed.

The transition from a segregated society to an integrated one proceeded with little difficulty in many ways; in others, the transition never occurred. By early 1970, a significant number of blacks worked side by side with whites on the production floors of local industries. Although a few "white only" signs remained posted on business entrances, the majority were removed. In most public places, both races occupied common space. Elsewhere, in churches, at social functions of restricted interest, and even within the larger mixed gatherings such as ball games and festivals, the mixture was minimal, but by choice rather than law.

After Chief Lister's health failed, forcing his resignation from the department, Captain James Hertford Parks Boozer followed Lister as chief in 1960. Boozer, a 1920 graduate of Greer High School, had moved into police work from mercantile trade. A clerk at Efird's Department Store, he later operated Payne Oil Company, a gas station, before entering police work. Before joining the police department in 1942, he had worked a year as a magistrate's constable. Boozer was records officer for the department for much of his career. Although his tenure was one of relative quiet, a single event brought Greer a degree of notoriety during his administration. Early in Boozer's administration, police escorted a Ku Klux Klan march through Greer. Klan members and families, including men, women, and children robed in white, red, and green regalia, remained after the parade, distributing literature and talking to the interested. The event garnered the attention of the media, which sent the story through the wire services across the country. Critical commentary appeared in distant editorials, condemning the police for their support of the Klan. Chief Boozer had done no more than give a minimal escort accorded to every parade conducted on the streets of Greer. Known for his effective administrative abilities, Boozer reorganized the department, hiring the first uniformed female auxiliary officers; Florence Belcher and Dorothy Cox were employed as uniformed crossing guards for school intersections.

David L. Belcher succeeded Parks Boozer as police chief in July 1968. Belcher, a grandson of a mill deputy and a state constable, was a graduate of Greer High and a Marine combat veteran of World War II. After he became a police officer in April 1947, he continued to be promoted, first to lieutenant in February 1960 and to assistant to the chief in December 1967. Belcher was the first Greer officer to complete the FBI's Law Enforcement Academy, graduating on November 5, 1968. Under Belcher's leadership, Greer employed its first African-American officer, Willie E. Wilson, and appointed Officer Dan Stepp as the first police detective. In 1971, the police department had 16 officers, 4 police-fire department dispatchers, and 4 crossing guards.

Police officers' salary scale was still an issue and began to have a greater effect upon employee retention. The average patrolman's pay was $105 per week when semi-skilled cotton mill workers were grossing $150 for the same six-day week. Belcher asked for a tax increase to raise officers' pay and retain officers who were leaving for work with other law enforcement agencies with higher pay scales. He proposed a police cadet program to aid recruitment and relieve patrolmen from desk duties for fieldwork. In terms of criminal investigation, Belcher was concerned with the emerging drug problem as early as 1965, contributing to state-level investigations in the Greer area and the promoting of the first local anti-drug educational campaign.

By the early 1970s, the police and fire department on Randall Street had outgrown its quarters. Both fire and police departments were operating out of the same office; a small courtroom was located upstairs across from the firemen's quarters. The two fire trucks were housed beside the office. In December 1974, the city signed a contract for the construction of a new facility to be located on the northwest corner of West Poinsett and Main.

Controversy erupted late in Belcher's tenure when the city council administrator, Lee Armor, restructured the city departments and employed a

*CHIEF BELCHER. Police Chief David L. Belcher addresses classmates at the FBI National Academy, Washington, D.C. 1969.*

civilian administrator as safety director over the police and fire departments. For the Greer Police Department, the year 1975 began auspiciously with two shootings, a robbery, and a fatal stabbing. Lee Armor, who became the city's first administrator in January 1975, focused his first attentions upon the operations of the police department. Armor brought representatives from the Law Enforcement Assistance Program (LEAP) of the Appalachian Regional Council of Governments to Greer to investigate police department recordkeeping. Armor's aggressive approach to his job resulted in many rapid changes in the way city departments performed their work. Lines of communication between department heads and city council broke down and became confused as Armor interspersed himself between city employees and his own employer, the city council. Investigators identified issues with police department operations which, when filtered through the media and local rumor mill, came across as accusations, precursory to formal charges. Chief Belcher defended the department and, in an informal meeting on March 19, demonstrated errors in the investigation. *The Greer Citizen* reported, "Recent statements which attacked the records system of the Greer Police Department and the integrity of its officers proved to be unfounded . . . " Practices cited by investigators were somewhat "Mayberryesque" by New York City standards, but were legal, honest attempts to accommodate local conditions. For example, some offenders were permitted to pay fines on the installment plan. Patrolmen shared ticket books.

Feeling ran high as Greer wrangled with the police department issue. As Greer became quickly divided over the matter, morale within the department declined. During the controversy, matters were complicated and tensions heightened by personal attacks against Chief Belcher. A caller (or callers) who eluded all attempts at a trace repeatedly threatened members of his family with physical harm. In mid-February, Belcher's watchdog was killed and his house and car riddled by gunfire. These incidents were never cleared. In mid-summer, Administrator Armor hired Jack Lister as public safety director. Lister had been one of the LEAP officials who began the investigation into police department operations. Citing "very little control over the operations of the Police Department" since Armor's arrival, Belcher took an early retirement in August.

The next two years were challenging for the police department as morale was low, personnel turnover increased, and criminal activity ran "rampant." Stability was tenuous, but a handful of older, experienced officers remained with the department. Detective Dan Stepp succeeded Belcher, but resigned at the end of July 1976 having never been "given the real command of the department." Lieutenant Alton Howard, the senior officer in the department, was made interim chief, but expressed no interest in the permanent job. Howard, working to restore public confidence in the department, used his long experience and dependability as an officer as an example to younger officers.

Issues and controversies continued to swamp the police department despite the forces of stability. Yet, in the long term, lessons were learned. The cost of the tumult was not merely a matter of hard feeling and personnel loss, but a loss of both public confidence and time for criminal investigation. Sixty criminal investigations were halted temporarily in mid-1976 when two detectives were suspended from the department. During the upheaval, at least two major investigations collapsed, one a murder, the other drug-related. The public recognized that the strength of the police department lies in its integrity and in the integrity of its leadership. By August 1976, as many as three-fourths of the citizens wanted the city administrator and public safety director removed. A Citizens Committee recommended the elimination of the position of public safety director and a reduction in the powers of city administrator. By that time, Greer had selected Kenneth Wayne Saylors as the new police chief.

An experienced officer with 20 years to his credit, Saylors came from Greenwood with impressive credentials, including a college education. Saylors' tenure marked a change of course for the Greer Police Department, as new issues appeared that had never before confronted them. Questions about the chain of command within the city government had not yet been resolved. The turnover rate was high, employee morale low. Not only was there a lack of public confidence, there was an increase of criminal activity similar to that found in larger towns. Marijuana and illegal drugs contributed a new set of related crimes, replacing alcohol-related offences as the number one problem.

By the mid-1980s, the police department employed 32 officers and operated 15 patrol cars, the increase in auto patrols suggesting the sprawling nature and attesting to provision of services to annexations, which by then had increased the city limit area to over 5 square miles. As the police department under Saylors and his successors dealt with these matters, two trends became evident: one was the increasing professionalism of the local department and the second trend was isolation of the department from the public it served. The open-door policy was discontinued at the new headquarters; foot patrol and contact with the public declined dramatically as Greer expanded far beyond its traditional limits.

From the late 1960s to the year 2000, changes in the business sector were stimulated by a number of factors. Greer benefited after the completion of Interstate Highway 85 and the location of the Greenville-Spartanburg Jet Port. The loss of the cotton and synthetic textile operations was mitigated by new and different industries locating in or nearby the city. Homelite, Celenese, and General Battery provided factory work at higher wages than mill hands had received. Availability of jobs within reasonable driving distance secured Greer's survival as an important hub in the late twentieth century, even if it altered traditional development and small-town atmosphere.

The directors of the Bank of Greer resisted affiliation with larger institutions for years, insisting that a strong, local independent bank could best serve the needs of the people it knew. New directions in banking demanded change, however, and the bank was absorbed by United Carolina Bank of South Carolina on October 1, 1986. Its expansion included seven branches with assets in excess of $150 million.

*THE NIGHT SHIFT. Officers Henry Sammons, Don Fisher, S.A. "Bill" Wall, Lieutenant B.A. Fincher, and David Belcher are photographed with a seizure of illicit whiskey. Five persons were arrested and 18 gallons of whiskey and a sawed-off shotgun were confiscated in October 1952.*

The last 30 years of the twentieth century saw growth along Wade Hampton Boulevard, extending in both directions. Attractive Greenville shopping centers were pulling traffic their way. Speaking to a chamber of commerce meeting, Phillip Hammer, a marketing specialist, predicted that the central location of Greer made it the site of an eventual mega-market, but warned, "the time for downtown action is now." Zoning was a major factor in keeping Greer's trade district as compact as possible, making it impossible to implement Hammer's recommendations smoothly and quickly. Zoning was generally opposed. One result of public reluctance to impose it was the sprawl of business along the principal traffic route, ultimately congesting the highway, which was intended for relatively unencumbered movement between Greenville and Spartanburg.

In early 1971, Greer's first modern shopping center was under construction. Grant Plaza, on Wade Hampton Boulevard, housed the W.T. Grant Department Store as the anchor business and a Winn-Dixie complete with deli and bakery, the first comprehensive grocery store in Greenville County. From the mid-1960s, downtown Greer declined as the center of commerce. Businesses either moved or closed; a revitalization attempt underway in 1981 included the construction of Square One, a planned open market place for farmers to sell their produce as available. The project was a nod to an enterprise passing from the scene; farming was already part of Greer's past when Square One was dedicated on October 3, 1981.

During the 1980s, Greer saw some firsts that displayed that the progressive town of the first of the century could reinvent itself to an inclusive community at the end of the century. The first African-American city councilman, H. Singleton Gilmore, and the first woman mayor, Shirley Rollins, were elected in the November 1987 elections and began their terms in January 1988. The Greer Family Festival that began in 1985 replaced the former Peach Festival. Yet, on the economic scene, the outlook was bleak as textile mills began to close and workers who had known no other way of life were without jobs.

After the last mill closed, people feared for the health of the local economy. Diverse companies had opened in Greer, but most employed small numbers. The building of the first North American BMW Plant between Interstate 85, Highway 101, and Brockman-McClimon Road brought new life to the area. Not only did the company provide more jobs, related industries moved nearby. People moved into the area, resulting in a building boom like none that Greer had ever seen. Mayor Don Wall, City Administrator Ken Westmoreland, and the city council became proactive in annexing areas until Greer, with 27 square miles, became the largest city in square miles in Greenville County. The 2000 U.S. Census counted 16,843 residents, making Greer the fastest-growing city in the state.

Increased population demanded better schools. Long-term school trustee Margaret Burch can be credited with new school buildings. By 2000, Greer had three high schools in the city limits: Greer High, Riverside, and J. Harley Bonds Resource Center for vocational studies, and new or completely renovated elementary and middle schools. Greenville Technical College located a satellite campus at the edge of Greer. In 1995, Greenville County Library replaced the old Davenport Memorial Library with the Jean M. Smith Library, a modern building with technology and materials for community use for the coming century.

Had not W.T. Shumate bought the Greer property and begun development in 1873, some sort of development mid-way between Greenville and Spartanburg still would have occurred, most likely with either Reidville or Pelham serving as the center of activity. Greer leadership and tenacity have served the community well over the years as it reinvented itself to give the city a personality of its own, never letting itself become a bedroom community of either Greenville or Spartanburg. A spirit of Modern Progressivism is evident as Greer meets the twenty-first century.

# Appendix

While likely an incomplete list, these Greer soldiers, sailors, and marines are known to have served their country during the Second World War:

Adams, Edward
Anderson, Fred
Andreas, Fred
Arnold, James
Atkinson, Bob
Bailey, Charles
Bailey, E.C.
Bailey, Julian
Bailey, Monroe
Ballenger, Warren
Ballentine, Carol
Barnett, Jimmy
Barnette, J.B.
Baswell James
Beeks, Brock
Belcher, Arnold
Belcher, Carl
Belcher, David
Belcher, John
Belcher, Ralph
Belcher, Thomas
Berry, Horace
Berry, Harold
Black Robin
Black, Clifton
Black, W.L.
Blackwell, Harold
Brady, Ellis
Brady, Marion
Brannon, Gus
Bright, DeWitt
Brockman, Harold
Brockman, Hiram
Brockman, Oliver Jr.
Brookshire, Paul
Brown, Preston
Bruce, Lee
Bruce, Robert
Bruce, W.L.
Burdrick, Samuel
Burgin, Hollis
Burgin, John
Burnett, Jack
Burnett, James
Burnett, Maud
Burnett, Willis
Cabiness Jack
Cabiness, Belt
Cabiness, Harry
Campbell, Lloyd
Campbell, Robert
Candler, Asa
Cannon, Raymond
Carman, Frank
Carman, Fred
Carman, Olin
Childress, Willie
Clarke, Charles

Clayton, Brooks
Cole, Alfred
Collins, Roy Jr.
Copeland, John
Cox, Haskell
Cox, Leroy
Cox, Roy
Cox, Wayne
Davis, Alvin
Davis, D.V.
Davis, Homer
Davis, Virgil
Dempsey, Marvin
DeYoung, R.B.
DeYoung, Theron
Digby, Mary
Dill, Brooks
Dillard, Thomas
Dixon, Aaron
Dobson, Bill
Dobson, Charles
Dobson, Clyde
Dobson, Dennis
Dobson, Roy
Duncan, Frank
Duncan, James
Duncan, Orvel
Edwards, Ralph
Edwards, Roy
Edwards, Vance
Ensley, Willard W.
Farmer, Alfred
Farmer, Jack
Farmer, Joe
Farmer, Malcolm
Few, Carlton
Finley, Joe
Fletcher, Charles
Forrester, Arthur
Forrester, Jack
Fowler, Ray
Frady, Hugh
Galloway, Charles
Ganett, Gordon
Gant, Roy
Gaul, Billy
Gibson, James
Giles, Theron
Glenn, Allen
Glenn, Robert
Godfrey, Samuel
Godfrey, Walter
Goodson, James
Gowan, Edgar
Green, J.O.
Green, James
Green, Marshall
Green, Olive
Green, Ralph
Green, Wilton
Hanvey, Maurice
Hardin, Melvin
Hardin, Wallace
Harrison, David
Harrison, George
Harrison, Woodrow
Harvey, Grady
Harvey, Louie
Hawkins, Jasper
Heath, Fletcher
Hemphill, Eugene
Hemphill, James
Hemphill, Sam
Henderson, Chester
Henderson, Everett
Henderson, Maurie
Hendrix, Charles
Hendrix, Theron
Hester, Harold
Hester, James
Hodgson, Ralph
Holtzclaw, Aldrige
Holtzclaw, L.S.
Holtzclaw, Stanley
Howard, Allen
Howard, Boyce W.
Howard, E.C.
Howard, Fred C.

Howard, Gurley
Howard, Harold
Howard, Leonard R.
Howard, Moulton C.
Howard, Samuel L.
Howard, William G.
Howell, Carl
Howell, Clement
Hughes, Bob
Hughes, Daniel
Hughes, David
Hughes, James
Ivie, Alonzo
Jackson, Don
Jackson, Paul
James, Laurens
Johnson, Helen
Jones, Albert R.
Jones, Frank
Jones, Harold Edgar
Kennedy, Winfred
Kirby, Melvin
Lancaster, William
Lane, William
Lanford, Marion
Lee, H.R.
Lee, Hubert
Lindsay, Ben H.
Littlefield, Raymond
Lowe, Perry
Lynn, W.T.
Mahaffey, Green
Manes, Milton
Martin, William
Mason, Paul D.
Mayfield, Ison
Mayfield, Louie
Mayfield, Murray
Mayfield, Norman
McAbee, Thomas
McCarter, J.T.
McCarter, Jewell
McCarter, O.R.
McCarter, Robert
Miller, Dan
Miller, Edwin
Moon, Brockman
Moon, William C.
Nabors, Pat
Neill, Eugene
Payne, John
Payne, Thomas Earl
Petit, Jack
Pruitt, Junior
Pruitt, Wilton
Putman, Grover
Reaves, H.D.
Rector, Frank
Rector, Fred
Rector, Grady
Rector, Murray M.
Riggs, D.E.
Robinson, William
Robinson, Don
Robinson, Joel
Rogers, Louis
Rumsey, Broadus
Rushton, Samuel
Sanders, Edward
Satterfield, Wi
Shepherd, David
Simms, Alexander
Sloan, Calvin
Sloan, Sidney
Smith Percy
Smith, Gordon
Smith, Hansel
Smith, J.W. Jr.
Smith, James
Smith, Milton
Smith, Norman
Smith, Tom
Smith, Vergil
Solesbee, Robert
Stansell, Dewey
Steading, Fred
Stokes, Ben
Stone, Carl

Suddeth, Theron
Taylor, Bruce
Taylor, Furman
Taylor, Gary
Taylor, Herbert
Taylor, Louie
Taylor, Roy
Taylor, Wilson
Thornton, Douglas
Thornton, William
Tucker, Henry
Tucker, Robert
Underwood, Charles
Underwood, Herbert
Vaughn, Alton
Vaughn, Boyce
Vaughn, Louis
Vaughn, Porter
Vaughn, Thomas
Vaughn, Tom
Wakefield, Walter
Walker, Anthony
Wall, Charles
Walls, Annie L.
Waters, Harold
Waters, James
Waters, Lupe
Westmoreland, John
White, Hubert
Williams, Daniel
Williams, Dewey
Williams, Robert
Wilson, S.V.
Winston, Petit
Wood, Buddy
Wood, Ethel
Wood, Jiggs
Wood, Louis
Wood, Proctor
Wood, Roy
Wood, William Esley
Woodward, Billy
Wylie, Fred

*GREER CHATAUQUA DAYS. The banner proclaims a Chatauqua Show during the 1920s. These traveling educational and entertainment shows began to appear in Greer after the turn of the century and were eventually supplanted by Vaudeville performances that were presented in theaters.*

# BIBLIOGRAPHY

## PUBLISHED WORKS


Batson, Mann. *The Upper Part of Greenville County, South Carolina*. Taylors, SC: Faith Printing Co., 1993.

Blackwell, Johanna DuBose. *A People and Their Faith: the History of Mount Tabor and First Presbyterian Church, Greer, South Carolina, 1841–1991*. Greer: First Presbyterian Church, 1991.

Camak, David English. *Human Gold From Southern Hills*. Greer: David Camak, 1960.

*Catalogue of Greer High School and Short Sketch of Greers, SC*. Spartanburg, SC: Trimmier's Book Store and Printing House, 1897.

*Clingstone*. Greer: Piedmont Heritage Fund, 1974–1977.

Flynn, Jean Martin. *An Account of Taylors, South Carolina, 1817 to 1994*. Spartanburg, SC: Reprint Co., 1995.

Greene, Anna. *A Short Sketch of the Town of Greers, SC, 1896*. Greer: Iris Clarke, 1937.

*Greenville Daily News*, 1874–1920.

*Greenville Democrat*. Microfilm. Parker Press, 1925–1928.

*Greenville News*, 1920–1964.

*Greenville Mountaineer*; *Greenville Enterprise*; and *Greenville Enterprise and Mountaineer*. Scattered issues on microfilm. Greenville County Library, 1838–1889.

*Greenville Piedmont*, 1927–1995.

*Greer Community Annual, Jan., 1927*.

*The Greer Citizen Centennial*, 1976.

*Greer City Directory 1915–1916*. Columbia, SC: Wing Publications, 1916.

*Greer Observer*, 1905–1918.

Hawkins, Ansel. "History of Woods Fort: An Address." A.M. Hawkins: Greer, 195?.

Huff, Archie Vernon. *Greenville: The History of the City and County in the South Carolina Piedmont*. Columbia, SC: University of South Carolina Press, 1995.

Jones, Lewis P. *South Carolina, A Synoptic History for Laymen*. Columbia, SC: Sandlapper Press, 1971.

Kinard, Joe Dew. *A Strong Tower: The Centennial History of the First Baptist Church of Greer, South Carolina, 1880–1980*. Greer: First Baptist Church, 1980.

Landrum, J.B.O. *Colonial and Revolutionary History of Upper South Carolina*. Greenville, SC: Shannon, 1897.

Paget, James Suddath. *Descendants of William Cunningham of Fauquier County, VA, and Greenville County, SC: 28 July 1770-14 Oct. 1853*. Greer: J.S. Paget, 2000.

"Pep." Senior Edition. Greer High School. Vol. V, No. 8. (May 1926).

Richardson, James M. *History of Greenville County, South Carolina: Narrative and Biographical*. Spartanburg, SC: The Reprint Co., 1980.

*Spartanburg Herald*, 1875–1982.

Snowden, Yates. *History of South Carolina*. Chicago: Lewis Publishing Co., 1920.

Taylor, Walter Carroll and Mary Moon Rawlinson. *Taylor Kinfolks*. West Columbia, SC: M.M. Rawlinson, 1975.

Teal, Harvey S. and Robert J. Stets. *South Carolina Postal History and Illustrated Catalogue of Postmarks 1760-1860*. Lake Oswego, OR: Raven Press, 1989.

Wallace, David Duncan. *The History of South Carolina*. New York: The American Historical Society, Inc., 1934.

## Unpublished and Private Material

Day Book and Farm Records of W.D. Ballenger, 1884–1900.

Greer Cotton Seed Oil Co. Daybook kept by Augustus Reid Wood. Strom Thurmond Institute Special Collections. Clemson University Clemson, SC: (22 December 1899 to 24 June 24 1902).

Ledger of W.M. Ballenger. City of Greer, SC: 1898.

Papers of J.J. McSwain. Private, unpublished.

## Public Records

City of Greer. Business Licenses, 1924–1928.

City of Greer. Minutes of the City Council, 1920–1965.

City of Greer. Ordinances of the Town of Greer, 1905, 1966, misc. 1902–1960.

Greenville County Court of General Sessions. General Sessions Courthouse docket microform. Greenville County, SC, 1845–1882, 1919–1931.

Greenville County, South Carolina, Records of Court of Common Pleas and Criminal Cases. Index to miscellaneous papers, microform, 1841–1885.

Greenville County, SC, Register of Mesne Conveyance Records of Deeds, Mortgages, Platts, Grants, 1838–1980.

Greenville County Estate Papers, 1787–1900.

Spartanburg County, SC, Records of Courts of Common Pleas and Criminal Courts.

Spartanburg County, SC, Register of Mesne Conveyance Records of Deeds, Mortgages, Platts, Grants, 1838–1980.

Spartanburg County, SC, Estate Papers, microform, 1787–1900.

State of South Carolina, Annual Reports of the State Superintendent of Education of the State of South Carolina.

Statues at Large of South Carolina. Columbia, SC: A.S. Johnston, 1836–1898.

# INDEX